KT-142-582

how to keep
houseplants
alive and happy

how to keep
houseplants
alive and happy

buying, growing
and displaying plants
in your home

peter mchoy

HERMES
HOUSE

This edition is published by Hermes House

Hermes House is an imprint of Anness Publishing Ltd
Hermes House, 88–89 Blackfriars Road, London SE1 8HA
tel. 020 7401 2077; fax 020 7633 9499
info@anness.com

© Anness Publishing Ltd 2005

All rights reserved. No part of this publication may be
reproduced, stored in a retrieval system, or transmitted in
any way or by any means, electronic, mechanical,
photocopying, recording or otherwise, without the prior
written permission of the copyright holder.

A CIP catalogue record for this book is available
from the British Library.

Publisher: Joanna Lorenz
Editorial Director: Judith Simons
Editors: Clare Nicholson and Elizabeth Woodland
Designer: Peter Butler
Jacket Designer: Whitelight Design
Photographer: John Freeman
Illustrator: King & King Associates
Production Controller: Claire Rae

Previously published as part of a larger volume, *How to Have
Happy, Healthy Houseplants*

1 3 5 7 9 10 8 6 4 2

Acknowledgements and Credits

The publishers would like to thank the following for
their generous help in the production of this book:
Andrew J Smith, Manor Nurseries, Stockbridge Road,
Timsbury, Hants, for providing plants, a location and
their time for much of the photography; Sean Flynn,
The Garden Studio, 146 Columbia Road, London E2,
for kindly lending a range of plant containers and
equipment featured in the chapter on Creative Displays;
Peter Watkins, Lease-a-Plant Ltd, M.K.M. Nurseries,
Bulls Lane, Bell Bar, Herts, for providing plants for
photography; The Dutch Nursery, Bell Bar, Brookmans
Park, Herts, for providing plants for photography;
The Camden Garden Centre, 2 Barker Drive, St
Pancras Way, London NW1, for lending plants for
photography; and The Chelsea Gardener, 125 Sydney
Street, Kings Road, London SW3 for providing plants
and containers for photography.

Special thanks are due to Stephanie Donaldson, who created
and styled the plant displays featured in the chapter on
Creative Displays; thanks also to Ann Venn, Nicky Walton
and Diane Redfern for kindly opening up their homes to
provide the settings for these plant displays.

All photography by John Freeman,
with additional photographs by Peter McHoy:
Key: t = top; b = bottom; l = left; c = centre; r = right.
Pages 20b, 22t, 24b, 25tl br, 26 b, 27tl tc tr b, 28t, 29b,
35t, 42, 43cr br, 55b, 56, 62br, 63, 65cl cr bl br, 86tr bc,
87tl tc bl, 88b, 89tr, 90bl br, 91tl tr bl, 72, 73tr, 74b, 75b.

Contents

Introduction

Some use houseplants purely as decorations, like ornaments or paintings on the wall, others treat them almost as botanical specimens, choosing examples of the native flora from every continent. However, if you want to get the best out of your houseplants, you need to appreciate them as plants as well as decorations and some understanding of the different plant groups will help you to display them appropriately and grow them more successfully. In the first chapter, *Discovering Houseplants,* you will find advice on how to recognize and use all the major plant groups around the home, along with tips on selecting the best plants for different positions.

However, be prepared to experiment with plants, accept that there will be failures, and look beyond the commonplace to discover the range of interesting or more unusual plants that you can grow in the home. Growing houseplants will then become an even more stimulating hobby.

The second chapter, *Caring for Houseplants,* will give you the advice and guidance you need to keep your plants in tip-top condition. Houseplants do, of course, demand time and attention. If you forget to water them, few will forgive the lapse. If you don't feed them, most will look weak and starved. None of this should deter anyone from growing them, for there are always plants and techniques that you can choose to suit the time you can devote to your plants.

For example, if watering is something you just can't remember to think about every day, or business or pleasure travel takes you away from home and there's nobody to plant-sit for you, there are simple solutions: concentrate on cacti and succulents that are naturally adapted to this kind of deprivation, or grow ordinary houseplants in special containers. Self-watering planters are ideal for groups of plants and you only need to top up the reservoir every week or so. Feeding is also easy with modern fertilizers. There are now slow-release tablets and sticks that you can push into the compost (potting soil) to release nutrients over a long period.

All these aids for the busy person are extremely useful, but caring for your plants can be a pleasurable part of growing them. By grooming them occasionally you not only notice whether pests are about to launch an attack, you also get to know your plants better, and often you will see things that would otherwise go unnoticed. If you do no more than slosh a bit of water onto your aspidistra you will soon take it for granted. But if you groom it by removing a dying leaf, or wiping the leaves over with a moist cloth to bring back the sparkle and gloss, you may suddenly notice a curious-looking purple flower sitting at compost level, a gem that you would otherwise miss. Houseplants are full of surprises, many of which only reveal themselves when you *really* care for them.

OPPOSITE: *A large specimen plant, such as this majestic palm, will make a statement in any home.*

RIGHT: *Plant groupings, such as these ferns displayed in a basket, create a stronger visual impact than single plants dotted around a room.*

Raising your own houseplants from seeds or cuttings can be extremely rewarding, and the third chapter, *Simple Multiplication,* offers clear advice on a whole range of different propagation techniques. Most houseplants can be raised from simple cuttings but, unlike hardy plants, the majority require warmth and humidity to root rapidly, so a propagator is a good investment. Apart from its use for cuttings, it will enable a whole range of seedlings to be started off in spring for both home and garden.

Lack of a propagator is only a restriction and not a bar to successful propagation. Seeds can be germinated in any warm location (provided that they are moved into a light position *without delay* as soon as the first ones have germinated). You can make a mini propagator by covering a pot with a clear plastic bag. Alternatively, a sheet of glass placed over a seed tray or a small cardboard box containing cuttings, can often work wonders with quite tricky plants.

Some people find propagation so fascinating that it becomes a hobby itself – with a constant search for new plants to try from cuttings or seed. Friends and neighbours are usually happy to spare a shoot or leaf from a plant that you take a fancy to, and looking through the seed catalogues for interesting houseplants to try is a pleasurable pastime.

The chapter on *Trouble-shooting,* is devoted to the problems you may experience in caring for your houseplants. Pests and diseases will undoubtedly occur from time to time. However, it should not be necessary to reach for potent sprays or to take drastic action such as discarding your plants as a first step. If a watch is kept for early signs of trouble when you groom the plants on a regular basis, pests like aphids can be eliminated before they breed and multiply.

ABOVE: *Nurseries and garden centres often offer a good selection of the more popular houseplants and some specialize in particular plants such as cacti and succulents.*

BELOW LEFT: *Collecting cacti and succulents can be a fascinating hobby. The examples shown here are, from left to right:* Echinocactus grusonii, Euphorbia milii *(syn.* E. splendens*) and* Opuntia vestita.

OPPOSITE LEFT: *Some plants, such as codiaeums, can be quite difficult to rear, but the challenge is worth pursuing.*

OPPOSITE RIGHT: *Bathrooms can be quite tricky locations for many plants, so be sure to select those that enjoy humidity.*

For example, many leaf diseases can be contained or eliminated simply by picking off any affected parts as soon as the disease is noticed. This will often prevent the disease from spreading and, more importantly, from releasing spores that will affect other parts of the plant or its neighbours.

While fast action is commendable, the overkill approach that resorts to a chemical armoury first is not always appropriate. If you want to avoid the use of chemicals completely, you can try a combination of good hygiene, vigilant hand picking and natural predators. You can buy predatory insects that parasitize pests such as whitefly, and although intended for use primarily in the greenhouse can be used indoors. They are useful in a conservatory, but natural control is not without problems: you have to accept a low level of pest infestation otherwise the predator dies out, and if you try to knock out the insects not controlled by the predator using insecticides that kill a broad range of pests, you will again upset the natural control cycle.

Sometimes plants fall sick for other reasons, such as nutritional deficiencies or physiological reasons. Plants that are pot-bound will look sick, and even too much feeding will cause symptoms of collapse that could be mistaken for pests or diseases affecting the roots.

You will find lots of ideas for using houseplants imaginatively in chapter 4, *Creative Displays*. There are suggestions for different rooms, and for ways in which you can use plants together so that one enhances the other. By using houseplants as ornaments, focal points and as integrated decorations in the home, you will derive even more pleasure from your plants than you would by regarding them merely as botanical specimens.

Although plants are constantly changing – they grow, die, or simply alter their shape – this very lack of stability can be turned to your advantage. Unlike any other decorative element that you can place and forget, and eventually even take for granted, plants have a dynamic existence. You have to move them, rearrange them, even repot them into different containers, all of which gives them an extra dimension and vitality that other kinds of ornaments lack. Flowering plants usually make a transient impact, but their use in internal design is no less powerful than that of the aristocratic yucca or tall ficus. You can choose flowers and backgrounds that

blend or contrast, to complement the mood you are trying to create.

Plants not only need to look good in a setting, they have to be happy there too. No matter how grand a plant looks in a rather gloomy corner of the room, it won't thrive, or even survive, if it needs good light. Plants that demand a humid atmosphere might survive in a kitchen but not in a living-room.

The creative displays used here should provide plenty of inspiration, but be prepared to experiment with your own ideas, to suit *your* tastes and *your* home. Above all, houseplants should please you and express your own personal tastes.

DISCOVERING HOUSEPLANTS

Growing houseplants should be a voyage of discovery, not only about the types of plants that will or won't grow well in your home, but also an exploration of the plant kingdom in all its diverse manifestations. You will get a lot more out of your houseplants if you investigate the potential of the various types of plants, and how they can be used in the home.

Dependable evergreens

CHOOSE SOME OF THE EASIEST AND MOST DEPENDABLE EVERGREENS AS THE
BACKBONE OF YOUR DISPLAYS. MANY OF THEM ARE TOUGH ENOUGH FOR
THE MORE DIFFICULT POSITIONS AROUND THE HOME, AND MOST OF THOSE
SUGGESTED HERE ARE BOLD ENOUGH TO BE FOCAL POINT PLANTS TOO.

The glossy evergreens such as dra-caenas, fatsias, ficus, scheffleras, palms and philodendrons generally make excellent stand-alone plants, but they can also be used as the framework plants for groups and arrangements. They will be far more robust than plants with thin or papery leaves, feathery and frondy ferns, or even those with hairy leaves. You need these other leaf textures, as well as flowering plants, to add variety of shape and form, and a touch of colour, but it makes sense to use the toughest evergreens as the basis of your house-plant displays.

Indoor 'trees'
Even the plainest room can be brought to life and given a sense of design and

character with a large specimen plant that has the stature of a small tree. Some houseplants grow into real trees in their natural environment, but in-doors you need plants that are in proportion with the dimensions of your room, and that won't quickly outgrow their space.

Large palms are ideal for this pur-pose, but many of the ficus family do just as well. The common *Ficus elas-tica*, once so popular, but now often passed by as unexciting, is a good choice, and there are many excellent variegated varieties that are far from dull. If you want an all-green one (and these have the merit of growing more quickly than the variegated kinds), 'Robusta' is a good variety to choose. If you don't like the upright and

TOP: Ficus elastica *was once a very popular houseplant, and is still well worth growing. The variety usually grown is 'Robusta', an improvement on the species that used to be grown years ago.*

ABOVE: Ficus lyrata *is a bold 'architectural' plant that can easily reach ceiling height.*

FAR LEFT: Philodendron scandens *is effective both as a trailing plant and grown up a moss pole, as here.*

LEFT: Yucca elephantipes *is a justifiably popular houseplant. It makes a bold focal point and is a really tough plant that should survive for years.*

sometimes leggy appearance of this plant, cut out the tip when it is about 1.5–1.8m (5–6ft) feet high, to stimulate low branching.

Other ficus to look for are *F. lyrata* (very large leaves with a distinctive shape), *F. benghalensis* (though the downy appearance of the leaves can make it a dull-looking plant), and the widely available *Ficus benjamina*. This is especially beautiful because it grows tall with a broad crown and arching branches. There are also beautiful variegated varieties of this species such as 'Starlight'.

Bushy plants that will give height and spread include *Schefflera arboricola* (syn. *Heptapleurum arboricola*) and *Schefflera actinophylla*. Both have finger-like leaflets radiating from a central point.

When a tough plant is needed

If you need a tough, glossy evergreen for a cold or draughty spot, perhaps for a hallway or near the back door, consider using some of the hardy foliage plants that have to cope with frost and gales when planted outdoors!

Fatsia japonica is another glossy evergreen with fingered foliage, rather like the palm of a hand (look for a variegated variety if you don't like the plain green leaves). Closely related is × *Fatshedera lizei*, a bigeneric hybrid between *Fatsia japonica* and an ivy. Grow it as a shrub by pinching out the growing tips each spring, or let it show its ivy parentage and grow more upright.

Others to look for are variegated varieties of *Aucuba japonica*, and *Euonymus japonicus* varieties such as 'Mediopictus', 'Microphyllus Albovariegatus' and 'Microphyllus Aureovariegatus'.

Ivies are ideal if you need a tough climber or trailer, and there are lots of varieties to choose from, with a wide choice of leaf shape, size and colour.

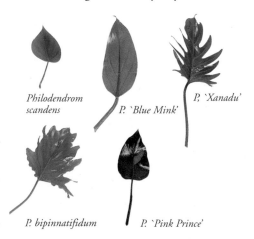

Philodendrom scandens

P. 'Blue Mink'

P. 'Xanadu'

P. bipinnatifidum

P. 'Pink Prince'

Philodendron leaves

Some genera have species and varieties with very different leaves, and they can make an interesting collection. The five philodendron leaves shown here are typical of the variation you can find within one group of plants.

TOP RIGHT: **Monstera deliciosa** *is one of the most striking focal point foliage plants that you can grow. The leaves are big and shapely, and the plant will grow large.*

ABOVE: **Scindapsus aureus,** *often sold under its other name of* Epipremnum aureum, *is a useful climber or trailer. This is the golden variety 'Neon'.*

ABOVE RIGHT: *Radermachera combines tough, glossy leaves with a 'loose' and almost ferny appearance; a refreshing change to most of the glossy evergreens.*

RIGHT: **Aspidistra elatior** *is a tough plant that seems to tolerate all kinds of neglect. If you look after it properly, however, you will have a fine foliage plant. There is also a variegated variety.*

Elegant palms

PALMS ARE THE EPITOME OF ELEGANCE AND WILL ADD A TOUCH OF SOPHIS-
TICATION TO YOUR HOME. THEY BRING TO MIND IMAGES OF A TINKLING
PIANO IN THE PALM COURT OF A GRAND HOTEL, YET SOME CAN LOOK JUST AS
ELEGANT AND IMPOSING IN AN ULTRA-MODERN HOME INTERIOR.

Many palms are slow-growing, and, consequently, large specimens are often expensive. But don't be deterred from trying palms; if you provide the right conditions, even small plants will gradually become impressive specimens.

Not all palms grow large, and many are compact enough for a table-top or for pride of place on a pedestal. Some are even small enough to use in a bottle garden while young. The box opposite will help you choose a suitable palm for a particular position.

How to grow healthy palms

The most common mistake is to regard all palms as lovers of hot sunshine and desert-dry air. They often have to cope with both in countries where they grow outdoors, but as houseplants you want them to remain in good condition with unblemished leaves.

- Keep cool in winter, but not less than 10°C (50°F).
- Keep out of direct sunshine unless you know that your palm revels in sunshine (a few do).
- Use a loam-based compost (potting soil) and ensure that the drainage is good (poor drainage is sure to cause problems).
- Only repot when absolutely essential as palms dislike root disturbance. Always ensure that the new compost is firmly compacted if you do repot.
- Water liberally in spring and summer, sparingly in winter.
- Mist the plants frequently with water and sponge the leaves occasionally with water.
- Do not use an aerosol leaf shine.

WHAT WENT WRONG

🔈 **Brown leaf tips** are usually caused by dry air. Underwatering and cold are other likely causes.

🔈 **Brown spots on the leaves** are probably caused by a disease, encouraged by overwatering or chills. Cut off all affected leaves.

🔈 **Yellowing leaves** are most likely to be caused by underwatering, though they could also indicate that the plant needs feeding.

🔈 **Brown leaves** are nothing to worry about if they are few in number and only the lowest ones are affected.

LEFT: *Washingtonia palms have fan-like leaves that create a striking effect.*

CHOOSING A PALM

❧ Tall and tough

Chamaerops humilis Can be grown outdoors where frosts are only mild; suitable for a cold position indoors. *Howeia forsteriana* (syn. *Kentia forsteriana*) and *H. belmoreana* (syn. *K. belmoreana*) Associated with the old palm courts. Will survive in a dark situation, but growth is very slow. *Phoenix canariensis* This one enjoys full sun (but beware of leaf scorch through glass) and can sit on the patio for the summer. Keep in a cool room – minimum about 7°C(45°F) – in winter.

❧ Table-top and easy

Chamaedorea elegans (syn. *Neanthe bella*) Can be used in a bottle garden when small. Insignificant flowers often appear on young plants.

❧ Difficult but worth the effort

Cocos nucifera This is the coconut palm, and it is usually grown as a novelty with the large nut clearly visible at the base. Even a young plant can be 1.8m (6ft) tall, and it is difficult to keep in the home. *Cocos weddeliana* A slow-grower. Can be used in a bottle garden.

ABOVE RIGHT: **Howeia belmoreana** *is sometimes sold under its other name of* **Kentia belmoreana.**

RIGHT: **Cocus nucifera** *is a big palm that is quite difficult to keep in the home.*

FAR RIGHT: **Chamaedorea elegans** *is a palm to choose if you want one that is easy and dependable. It will remain compact enough to use on a table-top.*

Dealing with brown leaves

It is natural for the lower leaves on palms to turn brown and die in time. To keep the plant looking smart, cut these off close to the point of origin (top). Secateurs (floral scissors) are adequate for most palms, but a saw may be required for specimens with very tough leaves. If the tips of the leaves turn brown, trim them off with scissors, but avoid actually cutting into the healthy leaf (above).

Variegated plants

VARIEGATED FOLIAGE PLANTS WILL BRING COLOUR AND A TOUCH OF THE
EXOTIC INTO A DULL CORNER OR BRIGHT WINDOWSILL, DEPENDING ON THE
TYPE. UNLIKE FLOWERING PLANTS, MOST REMAIN COLOURFUL FOR TWELVE
MONTHS OF THE YEAR.

Variegation has evolved for several reasons, and the two main ones are important to understand if you want to grow healthy-looking plants with good variegation.

Many variegated houseplants are derived from forest-floor dwellers in which variegation is useful where they occur in lighter areas, such as on the edge of clearings, because it reduces the area of functional leaf. This type of variegation is frequently white and green, the white areas cutting down the area that is reactive to sunlight. This group of plants often has the best variegation when positioned away from direct light.

Others are light-demanding species and have acquired colours and patterns for other reasons. Red and pink leaves are able to absorb light from different parts of the spectrum to green leaves, for example, and many different colours in the one leaf may make it more efficient. The variegation on these plants is often better if positioned in good light.

A few plants have colourful leaves to attract pollinators. The common poinsettia (*Euphorbia pulcherrima*), and bromeliads such as neoregelia, are able to change the colour of the leaves that surround the insignificant flowers from green to bright colours such as reds and pinks.

There are other reasons for variegation, such as a being a warning to predators, so there can be no simple rules that apply to all colourful foliage plants. Some, such as coleus and crotons (codiaeums) need bright light;

others like fittonias, with their white or pale pink variegation, must be kept out of direct sun.

Potential problems

Some plants lose their strong variegation if the light is too strong, others if it is too weak. If the plant seems unhappy, move it to a lighter or shadier position as appropriate.

If any isolated, all-green shoots appear on an otherwise satisfactorily variegated plant, cut them back to the point of origin. Some plants will 're-vert' and the all-green part of the plant will eventually dominate unless you remove the offending shoots.

Coloured bracts (the modified leaves that frame a cluster of flowers) will lose their colour or intensity of colour outside the flowering period. You can do nothing about this.

Begonia rex leaves
Although they are unlikely to be labelled as specific varieties, you can collect a whole range of *Begonia rex* with different variegations. Two other types of foliage begonias are shown here: *B. masoniana* (top left) and, to the right of this, *B.* 'Tiger'.

GOING FOR A COLLECTION

🍂 There are so many variegated houseplants that some people like to start a collection of a particular group of them. This makes it easy to provide the right conditions for all of them, and the searching out of new species or varieties to add to the collection adds another dimension to the hobby.

Good plants to collect are begonias (there are many variations among *B. rex*, but lots of other begonias have interesting variegation), caladiums (if you like a challenge), codiaeums, dracaenas and cordylines, marantas and calatheas, and pileas. Named varieties of vegetatively propagated coleus are difficult to obtain, but a packet of seeds will give you an amazing range of colours and variegation from which to select those to keep.

OPPOSITE TOP: **Begonia rex** *varies in leaf colouring from one plant to another, but all are attractively variegated and make bold foliage plants.*

OPPOSITE LEFT: **Cordyline terminalis,** *also sold as* **Dracaena terminalis,** *comes in many varieties, the difference being in the colouring and variegation.*

OPPOSITE RIGHT: **Dracaena marginata** *is a popular houseplant, and there are varieties with attractively variegated leaves.*

TOP LEFT: **Ficus benjamina** *'Starlight' is an outstanding houseplant with brightly variegated leaves on a plant that will eventually make a tall specimen with attractively arching shoots.*

TOP RIGHT: *Ivies (varieties of* **Hedera helix)** *are versatile plants that can be used as climbers or trailers.*

RIGHT: *Codiaeums, also known as crotons, can be demanding to grow well, but they make spectacular plants. Leaf hue and shape vary greatly according to variety, but all are bright and colourful.*

Graceful ferns

FERNS ARE FASCINATING PLANTS THAT WILL ADD A SPECIAL CHARM TO ANY
ROOM IN WHICH YOU WANT TO CREATE A FEELING OF COOL TRANQUILLITY
AND GREEN LUSHNESS. THEY BESTOW A RELAXED ATMOSPHERE IN CONTRAST
TO THE VIVID COLOUR OF BRIGHTER FOLIAGE PLANTS AND THE BRASHNESS OF
SOME FLOWERS.

Ferns are grown mainly for the grace and beauty of their fronds, and their elegance compensates for their lack of flowers.

The majority of ferns will thrive in shade or partial shade, conditions that are easily provided in any home. Unfortunately they also require lots of moisture and high humidity, both of which are in short supply in the average living-room. If you want ferns to thrive, you will have to choose easy and tolerant varieties (see the *Fern Selector* above right) or provide them with the humidity and moisture that is so vital. Although most of the ferns sold as houseplants come from tropical regions and benefit from warmth, central heating spells death to many of them unless you counteract the dry air by taking measures to increase the humidity, at least immediately surrounding the plants.

The ideal place for ferns is in a conservatory, porch or garden room where it is easier to establish a moist atmosphere.

Not all ferns need coddling, however, and some have adapted to dry air or cool temperatures. There are sure to be some ferns that you can grow successfully, and if you are determined to grow the delicate types with thin, feathery fronds, you can try planting them in a bottle garden or terrarium where they will thrive.

Starting with ferns

If you haven't grown ferns before, start with the easy ones. As you gain experience, add some of the more exotic and difficult species.

The commonest ferns are inexpensive, and even the more unusual kinds are usually cheap if you choose small specimens.

Florists and garden centres sell the most popular houseplant ferns, but you may have to buy the less common ones from a specialist nursery.

Propagating ferns

The simplest way to increase your ferns is to divide a large clump, or to remove offsets. Some, like *Davallia fejeenis,* send out rhizomes that root and can be used to grow new plants,

---

FERN SELECTOR

❧ Good for beginners
Asplenium nidus
Cyrtomium falcatum (syn. *Polystichum falcatum*)
Nephrolepis exaltata
Pellaea rotundifolia

❧ For the more experienced
Adiantum capillus-veneris
Platycerium bifurcatum
Polypodium aureum
Pteris cretica (and its varieties)

❧ Difficult but interesting
Asplenium bulbiferum
Davallia fejeenis

LEFT: *Most of the aspleniums are much easier to care for than the ferns with very thin and finely divided leaves.* Asplenium nidus *(left) has broad leaves that radiate from a central well or 'nest' and is a particularly good houseplant.*

Succulents

Succulents vary enormously in their requirements – some, such as semper-vivums, are tough and frost-tolerant, others are tender and temperamental. Always look up the specific needs for each plant, but as a rule they need very good light and little water in winter.

Displaying and collecting

Few cacti and succulents make good focal point plants – though a large epiphyllum in a porch can be a real stunner and they are generally best displayed as groups in dish gardens (shallow planters) or troughs. Cascading cacti, however, like the forest cacti already mentioned, are almost always displayed in isolation and look good on a pedestal while they are in bloom. But if you have a conservatory, you can try planting several of them in a hanging basket.

Cacti are very collectable, and you can grow literally hundreds of them in a modest-sized home. A frost-free greenhouse widens the scope considerably, and you can rotate the plants with those indoors, to maintain variety and interest.

Handling cacti

Repotting a cactus can be a prickly job. Make it easier on your hands by folding up a strip of newspaper or brown paper (top). Wrap this around the plant, leaving enough paper at each end to form a handle (above).

CACTUS OR SUCCULENT?

Succulent simply means a plant that has adapted to dry conditions and can retain moisture with minimal loss from its leaves, which are often plump and fleshy. Cacti are also succulents, but in all except a few primitive species the leaves have become modified to spines or hairs and the stems have taken over the function of leaves – being thick, fleshy and with the ability to photosynthesize.

Although most cacti have their natural home in warm, semi-desert regions of America, some grow as epiphytes on trees in the forests of tropical America. Some of these, such as zygocactus, schlumbergera and rhipsalidopsis, have produced hybrids and varieties that are popular flowering houseplants in winter and spring.

ABOVE: Crassula ovata, *like most succulents, is undemanding and will thrive with just a modicum of care.*

FAR LEFT: Euphorbia trigona *is an easy-to-grow succulent with distinctive three- to four-sided branches.*

LEFT: Sansevieria trifasciata *'Laurentii' is an attractive variegated plant that is really tough and needs minimal attention.*

Flowering houseplants

FLOWERING HOUSEPLANTS ARE USUALLY SHORT-LIVED IN THE HOME, BUT THEY BRING A SPLASH OF COLOUR AND VIBRANCY THAT NOT EVEN COLOURED FOLIAGE CAN ACHIEVE. THEY ALSO ADD AN ELEMENT OF SEASONAL VARIATION THAT FOLIAGE PLANTS LACK.

The most rewarding flowering houseplants are those that grow bigger and better each year, with each subsequent blooming crowning another year of good cultivation and care. Flowers that you should be able to keep growing in the home from year to year include beloperones, bougainvilleas, *Campanula isophylla*, clivias, gardenias, hoyas, *Jasminum polyanthum, Nerium oleander,* pelargoniums, saintpaulias, spathiphyllums and streptocarpus.

The disposables

Many flowering pot plants are difficult to keep permanently in the home and are best discarded when flowering has finished (or in some cases placed in a greenhouse if you have one). They are no less valuable indoors, and should be

regarded rather like long-lasting cut flowers. A lot of them are annuals and can, therefore, be inexpensively raised from seed: try browallias, calceolarias, cinerarias and exacums, which are all bright and cheerful, inexpensive to buy and not difficult to raise from seed yourself.

Annuals die after flowering and have to be discarded, but others are just not worth the effort of trying to

LEFT: **Begonia elatior** *hybrids can be in flower for most months of the year, but plants like the dwarf narcissus 'Tete-a-Tete' are especially welcome because of their seasonal nature.*

BELOW LEFT: *Varieties of* **Kalanchoe blossfeldiana** *are available in flower the year round.*

BELOW: *Pot-grown lilies make striking houseplants, but it is usually better to buy them in flower rather than try to grow your own from bulbs. Commercial growers can ensure that suitable dwarf varieties are used, and chemicals are often employed to keep the plants compact. Plant them in the garden to flower in future years.*

save in home conditions. Impatiens are often leggy if saved, and easy to raise or cheap to buy. Hiemalis begonias quickly deteriorate and are difficult to keep healthy. Furthermore, they are so cheap to buy that it's hardly worth taking up valuable space with them once flowering is over. Garden bulbs like hyacinths may bloom beautifully if forced for early flowering, but they will fail to give an acceptable repeat performance and are therefore best put out in the garden to recover and give a garden display in future years.

Hardy border plants such as astilbes are sometimes sold as pot plants. They look magnificent in flower, but the pot of large leaves left afterwards is hardly attractive, and the plant is almost sure to deteriorate if kept in-doors. By planting it in the garden after flowering you will have enjoyed plumes of beauty for a few weeks after purchase, then years of pleasure in the garden afterwards.

Tricked into flowering

Some plants are tricked into flowering at a particular time, or into blooming on compact plants. You won't be able to reproduce these conditions in the home. Year-round chrysanthemums are made to bloom every month of the

RIGHT: *Saintpaulias are among the most popular flowering plants, and there are so many variations in flower shape, size and colour that you can easily form an interesting collection of them.*

BELOW LEFT: *Hydrangeas make attractive houseplants if bought in flower, but they do not make easy long-term residents in the home. Try planting them in the garden when they have finished flowering.*

BELOW RIGHT: *Impatiens have always been popular houseplants, but the New Guinea types have bolder foliage than the older types usually grown. Some also have striking variegated leaves, as a bonus to the pretty flowers.*

year by having their day length adjusted by special lighting and by blacking out the greenhouse. They will probably be blooming on compact plants because they have been treated with dwarfing chemicals, the effects of which gradually wear off. If you manage to keep them going, they will become taller and probably flower at a different time. Try planting them in the garden – some varieties will thrive as garden plants if the winters are not too severe.

The poinsettia (*Euphorbia pulcherrima*) is another plant that is controlled by manipulating day length and in which height is also chemically controlled. Some people keep them successfully for future years, but they become taller plants, and the colourful bracts are produced at a different time of year unless their day length is controlled. This can be done by covering with a black polythene bag for fourteen hours a day for eight weeks. It is much easier to buy new plants.

Kalanchoes are also induced to flower outside their normal period by adjusting day length in the same way.

BRIGHT BERRIES

 Don't overlook plants with bright berries. These will often remain attractive for much longer than flowers; some of the most popular ones are easily raised from seed and are relatively inexpensive if you have to buy them. Annual peppers (*Capsicum annuum*) have cone-shaped fruits in shades of yellow, red, and purple. *Solanum capsicastrum* has orange or red berries shaped like small tomatoes – and with luck you can keep the plant going for another year, placing it outdoors for the summer. Remember to keep the air humid by misting periodically to prevent berries dropping prematurely.

OPPOSITE ABOVE: *Year-round chrysanthemums make excellent short-term houseplants. They are best bought in bud or flower then enjoyed for a few weeks before being discarded.*

OPPOSITE BELOW: *Berries can be as bright as flowers, and often last for much longer. Those of* Solanum capsicastrum *and* S. pseudocapsicum *and their hybrids look like cherry-sized tomatoes. The plants are usually discarded after flowering but can be kept for another year.*

TOP LEFT: Beloperone guttata *is easy to grow, long-lasting in flower, and you should be able to keep it from year to year.*

TOP RIGHT: Primula obconica *is a delightful houseplant when it is in flower. However, some people have an allergic reaction to the leaves.*

CENTRE RIGHT: *The azalea most commonly sold as a pot plant, and sometimes called* Azalea indica, *is botanically* Rhododendron simsii.

RIGHT: Euphorbia pulcherrima, *the so-called poinsettia, has insignificant true flowers, but really spectacular and colourful bracts to surround them.*

GARDEN ANNUALS

If you have a few spare plants after planting out the summer bedding, it might be worth potting some of them up into larger pots to use indoors. Among those that can make attractive short-term house-plants if the position is light enough are ageratums, lobelias, salvias and French marigolds.

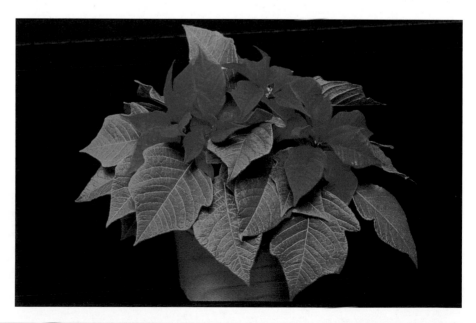

Scent in the air

SCENT ADDS ANOTHER DIMENSION TO YOUR PLANTS, AND IT'S NOT ONLY FLOWERS THAT ARE FRAGRANT. TAKE ANOTHER JOURNEY OF DISCOVERY WITH SOME OF THE AROMATIC HOUSEPLANTS THAT WILL MAKE YOU WONDER WHY YOU EVER USED CHEMICAL AIR FRESHENERS.

ABOVE: *The flowers of* Gardenia jasminoides *are pure white in full bloom, darkening to a creamy-yellow with age, and are richly fragrant.*

BELOW LEFT: Datura suaveolens *(syn.* Brugmansia suaveolens*) is a large and magnificent plant, with huge bell-like flowers and a strength of scent that matches the size of the blooms. This variety is 'Grand Marnier'.*

Perception of scent is an individual experience, and one that is more developed in some individuals than in others. Our ability to detect scents can be affected by the way in which our scent receptors are genetically determined. Some people are scent blind in the same way in which some people are colour blind. They can detect most smells but have a deficiency in certain types: someone who can smell a rose or a sweet pea might be unable to appreciate the equally potent perfume of the freesia. This makes it difficult to recommend specific plants to others without qualification: the plants suggested here have a smell readily detected by most people, but you may find a particular scent weak or even indiscernible.

Scent is further complicated by individual reactions to a scent when it is detected. Sometimes this may be for biochemical reasons, but it may even be that some scents are associated with pleasant or unpleasant experiences. There are scented-leaved geraniums (pelargoniums) that might remind one person of the tangy fragrance of lemons while another may detect a thymol smell in them that reminds them of an earlier visit to a dentist.

The only way to discover whether you like the scent of a particular plant

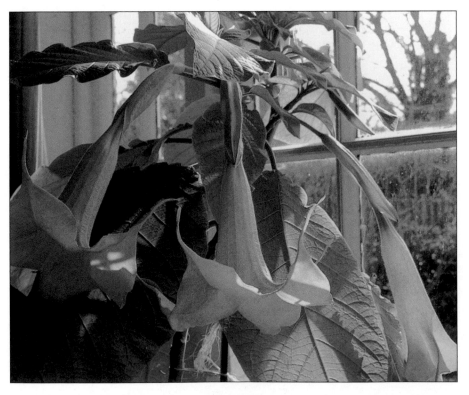

is to grow it and sniff it. You will almost certainly like those suggested below, but if you don't, simply cross them off your list for the future.

Placing scented plants

Plants that have a delicate fragrance, which you have to sniff at close quarters, such as an exacum, need to be positioned where sniffing is easy – perhaps on a table or shelf that you pass in the hall, or as a centrepiece for the dining table.

Plants with a dominant scent, like gardenias and hyacinths, can be so potent that one plant will fill the whole room with scent. It doesn't matter where you place these in the room, but avoid other fragrant plants that may conflict with them; place these in another room where you can appreciate their own distinct fragrances in isolation.

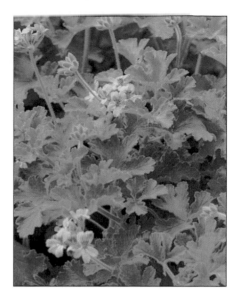

ABOVE: **Stephanotis floribunda** *is a very fragrant climber that can be grown as a pot plant while young.*

ABOVE CENTRE: *A bowl of hyacinths will fill a room with scent. Although they are at their best for perhaps a week, by planting different varieties, and using ordinary bulbs and those specially treated for early flowering, you can enjoy them over a period of months.*

ABOVE RIGHT: *Scented-leaved geraniums (pelargoniums) usually have insignificant flowers. Grow them for their aromatic foliage and position them where you might accidentally brush against them, or can touch the leaves to release their pungent fragrance. This is* Pelargonium graveolens, *with a scent reminiscent of lemons.*

BELOW: *Oranges make superb conservatory plants, and can be brought into the house for short spells.*

FRAGRANT FOLIAGE

🐾 Some of the best plants to grow for fragrant foliage are the scented-leaved geraniums (pelargoniums). These are just of few of them:

P. capitatum (rose-scented)
P. crispum (lemon-scented)
P. graveolens (slightly lemony)
P. odoratissimum (apple-scented)
P. tomentosum (peppermint-scented)

Plants that you have to touch or brush against to release the scent, like scented-leaved geraniums (pelargoniums), should be placed where you might come into contact with them accidentally, or intentionally, as you pass: alcoves or windows by a flight of stairs and on the kitchen table or worktop, for example.

SCENTED FLOWERS

🐾 Citrus (fragrant flowers, citrus-scented foliage and fruit)
Datura suaveolens
Exacum affine
Hyacinths
Hymenocallis × *festalis, H. narcissiflora*
Jasminum officinale
Narcissus 'Paperwhite'
Stephanotis floribunda

Orchids and other exotics

ADD A TOUCH OF CLASS TO YOUR COLLECTION OF HOUSEPLANTS BY GROWING
A FEW ORCHIDS, ALONG WITH OTHER EXOTICS, SUCH AS STRELITZIA, THE
'BIRD OF PARADISE FLOWER'.

Orchids have a reputation for being difficult to grow and, consequently, many people are deterred from trying them as houseplants. If you choose the right types, however, they are relatively undemanding and should make larger and more impressive clumps each year.

The drawback to orchids is the contrast between the beauty of their exotic flowers and the rather ungainly foliage with which you have to live for the other ten or eleven months of the year. The best way to grow them is to stand the plants in a sheltered and partially shaded spot in the garden during the summer – or better still in a conservatory if you have one – and then to bring them indoors for the winter or when they are coming into flower.

Easy orchids

The best orchids to start with are cymbidium hybrids, which are easy to grow, readily available and inexpensive to buy if you are not fussy about a particular variety.

Miltonias are a better choice if you want a more compact plant. The large, flat, pansy-like flowers come in a range of brilliant colours, and will often last for a month.

Cypripediums (paphiopedilums) are another group of distinctive and easy orchids to try. Sometimes called slipper orchids, the bottom petals form a slipper-shaped pouch.

Other orchids can be grown indoors, especially if you are able to create a special area for them, perhaps with artificial light, but it is best to gain experience first with the easy genera described above.

Other exotics

Try some of the following exotic-looking flowering plants that will bring some of the brilliance and flamboyance of the tropics to your home.

Anthuriums have vivid pink, red or orange 'flowers' that will never be ignored. The 'flower' is actually a spathe and it is the curly tail-like spadix that contains the true flowers. The 'flowers' are long-lasting and the foliage is attractive too.

Bougainvilleas are at their best climbing into the roof of a conservatory, but you could try one in a porch or light window. The bright 'flowers' are actually papery bracts. Prune after flowering and keep cool but frost-free for the winter.

Grooming orchids

With age, orchid leaves often become blemished. If the damage is towards the end of the leaf, try cutting it away. Angle the cut to make the end a more natural shape than if cut at right-angles.

Daturas are big plants, really at their best in a conservatory, although you can use small plants indoors. The huge bell-like flowers are usually white, pink or yellowish, depending on the species and variety. The heady scent matches the magnificence of the blooms, and even a single flower can almost fill a small house with scent in the evening.

Hibiscus rosa-sinensis grows into quite a large shrub but can be bought as a small plant. The blooms are big and beautiful: 10cm (4in) or more across, in shades of red, yellow and almost orange.

Strelitzias are sometimes called 'bird of paradise flowers' because the orange and blue flowers are thought to resemble the head of an exotic-looking bird. The leaves are often 1m (3ft) or more tall, and a large plant is truly spectacular.

HOW TO GROW ORCHIDS

❧ It is best to check the specific requirements for each species, but the following rules apply to most:

❧ Place them in a very light position, but not in direct, strong sunlight.

❧ Provide plenty of humidity. Stand the pots on a gravel tray, or mist regularly. Small plants do well in an enclosed plant case.

❧ Avoid draughts, but provide plenty of ventilation. Move them away from a cold window at night.

❧ Repot only when the pot is full of roots. Always use a special potting mixture recommended for orchids (you may have to buy it from a specialist nursery).

❧ Feed regularly during the summer.

❧ Stand the plants outdoors in a sheltered position for the summer if you don't have a conservatory to put them in.

❧ Water only when the compost (potting soil) is almost dry.

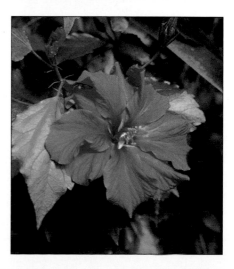

OPPOSITE TOP: **Strelitzia reginae,** *the 'bird of paradise flower', never fails to impress with its flamboyant flowers.*

OPPOSITE CENTRE: *The red or pink 'petals' that surround the insignificant proper flowers of the striking anthuriums are in fact modified leaves.*

TOP: *Bougainvilleas have a really exotic look, and although they are climbers can be used as a houseplant while small. Larger plants are best in a conservatory.*

ABOVE: *Phalaenopsis orchids will flower in most months of the year, but they are not easy plants to grow in the home.*

ABOVE RIGHT: *Cymbidiums are among the easiest orchids to grow in the house, but even so they usually benefit from a spell outdoors or in the greenhouse during the summer months.*

RIGHT: **Hibiscus rosa-sinensis** *blooms are big, bold and bright; they seldom fail to attract attention.*

CARING FOR HOUSEPLANTS

If you want your houseplants to thrive,
they need caring for and nurturing.
You have to choose and buy wisely,
understand the needs of individual
plants and make grooming a regular
job, just like watering and feeding.

Shopping for houseplants

SHOPPING FOR NEW AND INTERESTING HOUSEPLANTS CAN BE FUN, BUT BE WARY ABOUT WHERE AND WHEN YOU BUY. A PLANT THAT HAS BEEN POORLY TREATED BEFORE YOU BUY IT MAY ONLY REVEAL THE ILL-TREATMENT AFTER YOU GET IT HOME.

Choosing houseplants requires as much thought and care as the purchase of anything else for the home. Indeed, some plants will be with you for much longer than many household items.

You can buy a plant simply because you like the look of it, then try to find a suitable spot; or decide what you need to fill a particular niche in the home, before going out to buy an appropriate plant. The latter is undoubtedly the theoretical ideal, but it overlooks reality.

Except for the most common house-plants, the chances of finding a particular plant, even over several shopping trips, is not great and, more importantly, you may overlook a beautiful plant that you hadn't previously considered. Part of the fun of growing plants is to come across unexpected discoveries, plants that you've never seen before. Although advance planning is desirable, never be deterred from the impulse buy of something interesting or unusual, especially if you are prepared for a few failures along the way.

Where to buy

For everyday houseplants, a garden centre is often the best place to buy: there is likely to be a reasonable selection of 'basic' houseplants, and usually at least a few uncommon kinds. Most importantly, they will almost certainly be in conditions similar to a greenhouse: good light, warmth (ventilated in summer), with a buoyant and humid atmosphere. Staff are also

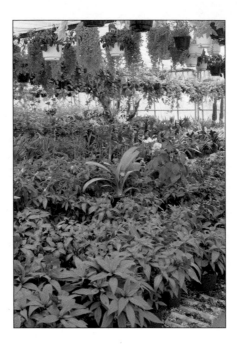

ABOVE: *Try to buy your houseplants from a nursery or garden centre where they have excellent growing conditions in good light.*

GETTING THEM HOME

🍂 Buy your plants last, immediately before you go home.

🍂 Don't put plants in a hot car boot (trunk), especially if you don't plan to drive straight home, or if the drive is a long one.

🍂 Make sure that they are wrapped in a protective sleeve if carrying them home by public transport. This will protect them from cold and wind, and guard against knocks.

---

usually knowledgeable, but beware of assuming that part-time or temporary staff know more than you do!

Florists also sell pot plants but, except for the very largest shops, the range is inevitably limited and conditions are seldom good. Some florists have pavement displays outside the shop, in which they include pot plants as well as cut flowers. Avoid these: you run the same risks as with market stalls (outdoor stands), where at least the price is usually cheaper.

Some large stores sell a limited range of plants. At the best of them the quality is excellent, with the plants well looked after and removed from sale if not bought within a certain time. In others they can languish in poor light and with inadequate care, slowly deteriorating until they reach the point of death. The quality and condition of plants sold by ordinary shops or home-improvement stores vary enormously. Go through the *Buyer's checklist* below carefully before buying from these sources.

Market stalls often sell plants at very competitive prices, and they are usually sold quickly, so it is possible to obtain quality plants cheaply if you don't mind the limited range. Beware of buying in cold weather – especially in winter. The chill plants receive, having come out of hot-house conditions, may not be obvious until a few days after you get them home, when the leaves start to drop. Even in the summer, houseplants displayed outdoors can suffer a severe check to growth if the weather is cold or windy.

Buyer's checklist

- Check the compost (potting soil). If it has dried out the plants have been neglected. Don't buy.
- Lift and check the base of the pot. If lots of roots are coming out of the bottom, the plant should have been repotted sooner. A few small roots through the bottom of the pot is not a sign of neglect, and is normal where the plants have been grown on capillary matting.

- If buying a flowering plant, make sure that there are still plenty of buds to open, otherwise the display may be brief.
- Look critically at the shape. If growth is lop-sided, or the plant is bare at the base, choose another.
- Make sure the plant is labelled. A label should tell you how to care for the plant, and unlabelled plants suggest a lack of concern for plants and customers.
- Avoid plants with damaged or broken leaves.
- Don't be afraid to turn the leaves over. Look for signs of pests and diseases. If you find any, leave them in the shop!
- If the plants are displayed in a protective sleeve, don't buy unless you can remove your potential purchase for inspection. Display sleeves can hide all kinds of horrors, such as rots and diseases, pests, and even a sparse or poorly shaped plant.

Protective sleeves

These can be useful: they help to get the plant home with minimum damage and offer some protection from cold winds in winter. But make sure they don't hide damaged or diseased leaves. Be prepared to remove the sleeve to examine a plant if they are displayed in this way.

Root check

It is natural for a few roots to grow through the bottom of the pot, especially if a capillary watering system has been used (which is normal in plant nurseries), but a mass of roots growing through the pot is probably a sign that the plant needs repotting.

Flowering plants

When buying a flowering plant, make sure that there are plenty of buds still to open. A plant in full flower may be more spectacular initially, but the display will be shorter.

Pests and diseases

Examine the undersides of a few leaves to make sure they are free of pests and diseases before you buy.

Pot sizes

Houseplants look better, and will grow better, if they are in a pot of an appropriate size. The plant in the picture at the top of the page is in a pot that's too large – it dominates the plant. The one shown above is in a pot that's too small; not only is it top-heavy and unstable, but the amount of compost (potting soil) in the pot is unlikely to be sufficient to sustain the plant.

Creating the right environment

IT'S IMPOSSIBLE TO RECREATE THE ATMOSPHERE OF A SOUTH AMERICAN RAINFOREST OR THE SEMI-DESERT CONDITIONS OF THE WORLD'S MORE ARID REGIONS IN OUR HOMES. YET WE EXPECT ORCHIDS AND BROMELIADS TO THRIVE ALONGSIDE CACTI AND SUCCULENTS, PLANTS FROM THE WORLD'S WARMEST REGIONS TO COEXIST WITH HARDY PLANTS SUCH AS IVIES AND AUCUBAS. CREATING THE RIGHT CONDITIONS TO SUIT SUCH A DIVERSITY OF PLANTS, WHILE KEEPING A HOME THAT'S ALSO COMFORTABLE TO LIVE IN, CALLS FOR INGENUITY AND A DASH OF COMPROMISE.

Use the advice on labels and in books as a guide to the best conditions in which to keep your plants. In reality you may not be able to accommodate all the conditions listed as desirable, but most plants will still survive even if they do not thrive. Take recommendations for humidity seriously: a plant that requires very high humidity is likely to die soon in very dry air. Recommendations regarding light and shade are important but if you get this slightly wrong the consequence is more likely to be poor variegation, perhaps scorch marks on the leaves, or drawn and lanky plants, rather than dead ones. You can usually correct the problem by moving the plant.

Temperature is the most flexible requirement, and most plants will tolerate a wide fluctuation above or below the suggested targets.

Temperature
Treat with caution advice in books and on labels that gives a precise temperature range. Most plants will survive temperatures much lower than the ones normally recommended, and, in winter when the light is poor, a high temperature may stimulate growth that can't be supported by the light levels. Upper temperature figures are meaningless unless you have air conditioning. In summer the outside temperature often rises above those recommended for particular plants, and unless you have some way of cooling the air, the plants will have to suffer the heat along with you. They will almost certainly come to no harm if shaded from direct sun and provided that the humidity is high enough.

Once the temperature drops towards freezing, however, most houseplants are at risk. Even in a centrally heated home, temperatures can drop very low if heating is turned off at night.

Light and shade
The best position for most plants is in good light but out of direct sun. Even plants that thrive in sun outdoors may resent the strongly magnified rays through glass, which will often scorch the leaves. Be especially wary of positioning plants behind patterned glass in full sun: the pattern can magnify the sun's rays.

Only plants that normally grow in deserts, on steppes, high mountains and barren moors grow in areas devoid of shade. And even these may not like the sun's rays intensified through glass. If possible, fit shades that you can use for the hottest part of the day. Even net curtains are useful in screening out some of the strongest rays.

The so-called shade plants do not like any direct sun, but that does not necessarily mean that they will grow in gloom. The eye is deceptive when it comes to judging light levels. Use a camera fitted with a light meter, and measure the light in different parts of the room. You might discover that the light is as poor immediately above or below a window as it is in the centre of the room. If the windows are high, experiment with the light meter to see how much better the light might be if

Effects of heat
Leaf scorch (brown marks or blotches that leave the areas looking thin and papery) is a common problem on plants placed on a very sunny windowsill. Unless they are adapted to this kind of intense heat, the tissue of the leaves can be damaged. The problem is most likely if drops of water are left on the foliage in bright sunlight (the water acts like a magnifying glass) or where patterned glass intensifies the sun's rays as it acts like a lens.

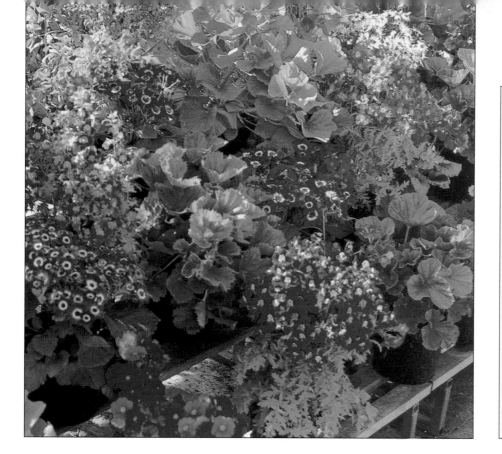

> ### KEEPING THEM INSULATED
>
> ❧ The greatest dangers to plants are cold draughts, especially at night when the temperature drops and the heating is turned off, and frost. Take precautions to keep them insulated:
>
> ❧ Move plants into the room when you pull the curtains – don't leave them trapped between curtains and glass, where the temperature can drop dramatically.
>
> ❧ If you have to leave plants by a window on a cold night, try insulating them with sheets of polystyrene (styrofoam) placed against the lower half of the window.

you raised a plant on a pedestal or positioned it on a low table.

Humidity

Humidity – or the amount of moisture present in the air at a given temperature – is important to all plants, but especially those with thin or delicate leaves, such as ferns, selaginellas and caladiums. Grow those plants that need a very humid atmosphere in a bottle garden or plant case, or mist the plants frequently (at least once a day, more often if possible).

For less demanding plants that still need high humidity, grow them in groups to create a microclimate or stand the plants on gravel, pebbles or marbles in a shallow dish containing water. Provided that the bottom of the pot is not in direct contact with the water the air will be humid without the compost becoming waterlogged. Misting is still desirable, but if the plants are in flower shield the blooms while you do so, otherwise the petals may become marked or begin to rot.

Simple humidity trays to place over radiators are inexpensive and help to create a more buoyant atmosphere for houseplants.

ABOVE: *Plants like schizanthus and cinerarias will make a super show if you can provide good light and humid conditions.*

Increasing humidity
It can be difficult to create a humid environment in the home, but a small microclimate can be created around the plant. Standing the plant over a dish containing water will increase the humidity, but the pot must be stood on small pebbles or marbles to keep it above water level and avoid waterlogged compost (potting soil).

Misting foliage plants
The majority of houseplants will benefit from misting with water. If you can do it daily the plants will almost certainly grow better. Delicate ferns that need a very high humidity may need misting several times a day for really good results

Misting flowering plants
Although the foliage benefits from misting, water can damage delicate flowers. Simply protect the blooms with a piece of paper or cardboard if the plant is in flower.

Windowsill plants

WINDOWSILLS ARE A FAVOURITE POSITION FOR HOUSEPLANTS, BUT YOU NEED TO CHOOSE PLANTS APPROPRIATE TO THE ASPECT. NOT ALL PLANTS APPRECIATE A BAKING IN THE SUNSHINE.

ABOVE: Hoya carnosa *is a pretty climber or trailer for a sunny position. It is usually grown for its white flowers, but the variegated 'Tricolor' also makes an attractive foliage plant.*

It is a good idea to analyse the amount of direct light coming through each window before deciding on the best spots for various plants with different light needs. Large windows obviously let in most light, but it will still be less than outdoors, and the larger the area of glass, the more rapidly temperatures drop at night.

The majority of plants flourish best when placed in good light in a position that is shaded from the direct rays of the sun. There are bound to be some rooms that receive little direct light, but most will receive some sun at least in the morning or evening. Except for shade lovers that are particularly vulnerable to direct sun, the majority of plants will benefit from this as the strength of the sun is generally weaker in the early morning and evening, so leaf scorch is less likely. The compost (potting soil) is also less likely to dry out rapidly if the sun has moved around before its midday peak.

Very sunny windows can still be packed with interest if you select the plants carefully, but be prepared to keep the compost well watered in warm weather. Avoid splashing the leaves when the sun is on them, however, as the droplets of water can act like a further magnifying glass and scorch the leaves.

The lists of suggested plants given here are not definitive, but an example of what can be grown. Be prepared to experiment with many more, especially on a light windowsill that does not receive fierce direct sun.

Where only the genus is mentioned, all the widely available species sold as houseplants should be successful.

You will find some plants listed in more than one group. Many plants will grow in sun or partial shade and a few will do well in both direct sun and indirect light.

Plants for a very sunny window

Ananas, cacti, ceropegia, chlorophytum, coleus, geraniums (pelargoniums), regal, zonal, scented-leaved, gerbera, hippeastrum, *Hoya carnosa,* hypocyrta, impatiens, iresine, *Kalanchoe blossfeldiana* and hybrids, nerium, *Plectranthus fruticosus,* sansevieria, setcreasea, stapelia, succulents (most), yucca and zebrina.

Plants for a window that receives early or late sun

Aechmea, aglaonema, anthurium, aphelandra, begonia, beloperone, billbergia, caladium, calathea, capsicum, chlorophytum, chrysanthemum, cocos, codiaeum, coleus, *Cordyline terminalis* (syn. *C. fruticosa*) and varieties, crossandra, cuphea, ficus (most), gardenia, gynura, hoya, impatiens, maranta, nertera, *Plectranthus oertendahlii,* rhipsalidopsis, saintpaulia, sansevieria, sinningia, solanum, spathiphyllum, tolmiea, tradescantia, zebrina.

Plants for a light window out of direct sunlight

Adiantum, aglaonema, anthurium, asparagus, aspidistra, asplenium, billbergia, calathea, chlorophytum, clivia, dieffenbachia, dracaena, ferns, *Ficus deltoidea, Ficus pumila,* hydrangea, maranta, orchids, saintpaulia, sansevieria, selaginella, soleirolia (syn. helxine), spathiphyllum.

ABOVE: Aphelandra squarrosa *needs good light but not direct summer sun. Grow it where it just receives early or late sun in the summer and in the best light possible in winter.*

ABOVE: *Gerberas will tolerate a very sunny position, but if you plan to discard the plant after flowering you can use it to brighten up dull spots too.*

ABOVE: **Mammillaria elongata**, *like most cacti, will thrive in a hot, sunny position.*

ABOVE: **Calathea zebrina** *is best in a light position that receives early or late sun, but not direct midday sun.*

ABOVE: **Aglaonema** *'Silver Queen' grows well in semi-shade or bright light, but avoid direct midday sun.*

ABOVE: **Yucca elephantipes** *benefits from as much light as possible. It will enjoy a hot, sunny position.*

BELOW: **Zygocactus (Schlumbergera)** *hybrids are forest cacti, best grown in good light shaded from direct sunlight.*

ABOVE: **Aechmea fasciata** *is grown mainly for its fascinating flower spike. Because it grows naturally in trees, it is not adapted to life on a very hot, sunny windowsill. Position it where it receives early or late sun.*

ABOVE: **Sansevieria trifasciata** *'Laurentii' is one of those tough plants that will do well on any windowsill, in shade or full sun.*

RIGHT: **Kalanchoe blossfeldiana** *hybrids do well on a sunny windowsill.*

Shady spots

PLANTS THAT TOLERATE SHADE ARE PARTICULARLY USEFUL, ESPECIALLY IF YOU NEED FOCAL POINT PLANTS FOR DIFFICULT POSITIONS WITHIN THE ROOM. LARGE SPECIMEN PLANTS ARE USUALLY TOO LARGE FOR A WINDOW-SILL SO THESE HAVE TO COMBINE SIZE WITH SHADE TOLERANCE.

It is a mistake to position a plant purely for decorative effect, and you should always choose a spot that the plant will at least tolerate even if it doesn't thrive. For really inhospitable corners where it's just too dark even for shade lovers, use disposable flowering plants, or even ferns if you are prepared to discard them after a couple of months.

In winter, plants are unlikely to tolerate a light intensity less than 1,000 lux, and 5,000 lux in summer is about the minimum for foliage plants such as aspidistras and *Cissus rhombifolia* (syn. *Rhoicissus rhomboidea*). These are meaningless figures unless you have a way of measuring light, but fortunately there is a simple rough-and-ready way that can be used. Two methods of judging light levels are described in *How to Assess Light* (opposite).

ARTIFICIAL LIGHT

Artificial light can be used to highlight plants in dull spots, and can also be used to help plants thrive where natural light is inadequate.

Even ordinary light bulbs can help plants to grow by providing localized warmth and a degree of increased illumination. However, fluorescent tubes are better for plant growth and, because they generate less heat, they can be used closer to the plant. Light sources need to be close, and if possible the tubes should be specially balanced for plant growth (you can buy these at some gardening shops and also at aquarium suppliers). Otherwise use the tubes in pairs with one 'daylight' and one 'cool white' used together.

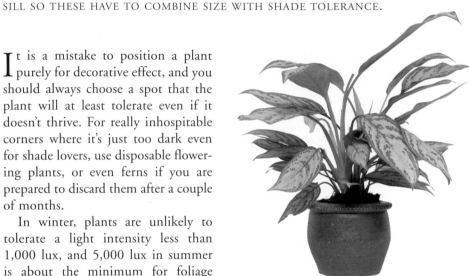

ABOVE: **Aglaonema** *'Silver Queen' is undemanding and useful for low-light areas.*

ABOVE: **Aucuba japonica** *varieties are not only shade-tolerant but cold-tolerant too. They are frost-hardy, so choose them for a position that has both low light levels and low temperatures in winter.*

ABOVE: **Ficus pumila** *is a low-growing trailer that would soon die on a sunny window. The variegated varieties are more attractive than the all-green species.*

ABOVE: **Fatsia japonica** *is a garden shrub hardy enough to grow outside except in very cold regions, but indoors the variegated form is more attractive. Choose it for a low light area where temperatures also drop in the winter.*

ABOVE: **Philodendron scandens** *is a useful trailer for a low-light area.*

ABOVE: Helxine soleirolii, *also sold as*
Solierolia soleirolii, *is a tough carpeter
that will tolerate low light and cool
temperatures (it will even stand some frost).
There are green, silver and golden forms.*

ABOVE: *Ivies (varieties of* Hedera helix*)
grow happily in the wild in sun or shade,
and they will do the same in the home. If
possible provide bright conditions in winter
and avoid direct sunlight in summer.*

ABOVE: Fittonia verschaffeltii *is one of the
more difficult foliage plants to try. It will
be short-lived in direct sunlight.*

ABOVE: Pellaea rotundifolia *does not
demand such a humid atmosphere as most
ferns; a light window out of direct sunlight
is ideal.*

ABOVE: Adiantum capillus-veneris *will
not tolerate a hot, sunny position for long.
It will be much happier in a humid and
shaded conservatory.*

ABOVE: Scindapsus aureus, *also sold as*
Epipremnum aureum, *is a trailer or
climber that will do well in low-light areas.
This golden form is particularly bright,
but in time the leaves become more green
and less colourful.*

ABOVE: Asplenium nidus *is one of the
easiest ferns to grow.*

HOW TO ASSESS THE LIGHT

❧ Use a camera with a built-in light
meter, and set it to a 100 ISO (ASA)
film speed and 1/125 second shutter
speed. Take the reading at about
midday on a bright day in late spring
or early summer. Position the camera
where you want to place the plant,
and point it towards the window.

Read off the aperture setting then
use the following as a rough guide to
the light level:

f16 or more = Strong light,
suitable for those plants that need
the best light.

f8–11 = Equivalent to screened
daylight, and suitable for those
plants that like good light but not
strong direct sunlight.

f4–5.6 = Poor light, only suitable
for those plants adapted to shade.

f2.8 = Suitable for only the most
shade-tolerant species, and plants
may not survive in the winter
months.

❧ Another test is to try reading
a newspaper where you plan to
position the plant. Assuming that
you have good eyesight, the position
is too dark for plants if you can't read
the newspaper comfortably.

❧ **Plants for poor light**
Aglaonema, araucaria, asplenium,
aspidistra, aucuba, bulbs (such as
hyacinths), but keep in good light
until flowering starts, *Cissus
rhombifolia* (syn. *Rhoicissus rhomboidea*)
× Fatshedera, fatsia, ferns (most),
Ficus pumila, fittonia, *Hedera helix*
(ivy), palms (most), *Philodendron
scandens,* pteris, sansevieria,
Scindapsus aureus (syn. *Epipremnum
aureum, Rhaphidophora aurea),* but be
prepared for it to lose most of its
variegation, *Soleirolia soleirolii* (syn.
Helxine soleirolii).

Watering

NO PLANT CAN SURVIVE WITHOUT WATER, YET MORE PLANTS PROBABLY DIE FROM OVERWATERING THAN FROM UNDERWATERING. GETTING TO GRIPS WITH THE BEST TECHNIQUES AND HOW OFTEN TO DO THIS SIMPLE PROCEDURE IS ONE OF THE ESSENTIALS OF GOOD PLANT CARE.

Compost (potting soil) check

If you use a clay pot, it will ring with a hollow sound if you tap it with a cotton reel on a cane or pencil and the compost is dry. If the compost is still moist the sound will be duller. With a little experience you will be able to detect the difference.

Meters and indicator strips that are pushed into the compost help to put some kind of measurement to the amount of moisture available in the compost, but are impractical if you have a lot of houseplants. You will soon tire of pushing a probe into each pot or reading indicators left in each one. These devices are best used by beginners still gaining experience of how to judge the moisture content by other means.

How much water?

There are no fixed rules about watering. How much a plant needs, and how often, depends not only on the plant but also the kind of pot (clay pots need watering more often than plastic ones), the compost (potting soil), (peat-based composts retain more water than loam-based), and the temperature and humidity.

Watering is an acquired skill, and one that needs to be practised on an almost daily basis, otherwise it is best to switch to self-watering containers or hydroponically grown plants.

Useful techniques

Examine the pots daily if possible, using whichever of the following techniques you find the most convenient:

- Appearance alone can be a guide. Dry, loam-based composts (potting soils) look paler than when they are moist. A dry surface does not mean that the compost is dry lower down, but if it looks damp you know that you don't need to

water. If the plant is placed in a saucer, see if there is any standing water. Apart from bog plants, never add more water if there is any trace still left in the saucer.

- The touch test is useful for a peat-based compost. Press a finger gently into the surface – you will know immediately if it feels very dry or very wet.
- The bell test is useful for clay pots, especially large ones containing specimen plants and that hold a large volume of compost. Push a cotton reel onto a short garden cane

Watering from above

A small watering-can is still the most popular way to water houseplants. Choose one that is well-balanced to hold and with a long, narrow spout that makes it easy to direct the water to the compost (potting soil) rather than over the plant.

and tap the pot: a dull thud indicates moist compost (although it could also indicate a cracked pot!), a clear ring suggests dry compost. This doesn't work well with peat-based composts, and not at all with plastic pots.

- With practice you can tell when the compost is dry simply by lifting the pot slightly: a pot with dry compost will feel much lighter than one with moist compost.

How to water

When you water, fill the pot to the brim – dribbles are not sufficient. If the root-ball has completely dried out, water may run straight through, down the inside of the pot, in which case stand the pot in a bucket of water until the air bubbles stop rising.

After watering, always check whether surplus water is sitting in the saucer or cache-pot. This will not matter if there are pebbles or marbles to keep the bottom of the pot out of contact with the moisture, but otherwise you must tip out the extra water. *Failure to tip out standing water is the most common cause of failure.* With just a few exceptions, if you leave most ordinary houseplants standing in water for long, they will probably die.

A long-necked watering-can is the most convenient way to water the majority of houseplants. The long neck makes it easy to reach among the leaves, and a narrow spout makes it easier to control the flow, which is also less forceful and unlikely to wash the compost (potting soil) away.

Watering with a can means that you may wet the leaves and crown of ground-hugging plants such as saintpaulias, and unless you are careful this can encourage rotting. For plants like this you may prefer to stand them in a bowl with a few centimetres (inches) of water in the bottom. Remove and allow to drain as soon as the surface of the compost becomes moist. You will probably find it less trouble, however, to be careful with a long-necked watering-can, getting the spout beneath the leaves.

Special needs

Tap water is far from ideal, but the vast majority of houseplants will tolerate it. If the water is hard (has a high calcium or magnesium content), however, you need to make special arrangements for plants that react badly to alkaline soil or compost. These include aphelandras, azaleas, hydrangeas, orchids, rhododendrons and saintpaulias. Rain-water is usually recommended for these plants, but a good supply is not always available throughout the year, and in some areas it can be polluted.

If your tap water is only slightly hard, simply filling the watering cans the day before and allowing the water to stand overnight may be sufficient. For harder water, try boiling it: part of the hardness will be deposited in the form of scale, and you can use the water once it has cooled.

Many water softeners work on a principle that unfortunately does not help the plants: if you want to benefit the plants, a demineralization system is necessary, which removes all the minerals and leaves distilled water. However, it is only worth the expense if you have a lot of plants.

If a plant wilts or collapses like this (top) it can usually be revived by standing the pot in a bowl of water for a few hours, then leaving it in a cool, shady position for a day. By the next day it will probably be as perky as before (above). Always make sure that the compost (potting soil) is dry before doing this, as an overwatered plant will also wilt.

Watering the outer pot
Just a few plants tolerate standing with their roots in water, like this cyperus. With these you can add water to the saucer or outer container, but never do this unless you know the plant grows naturally in marshy places.

Self-watering pots
If you find watering a chore, self-watering pots may be the answer. The moisture is drawn up into the compost (potting soil) through wicks from a reservoir below, and you will need to water much less frequently.

Overwatering
Before an overwatered plant reaches the stage of collapsing, it will probably begin to look sickly. The plant on the left has been overwatered, the one on the right has received the correct amount of water.

Feeding

FEEDING CAN MAKE THE DIFFERENCE BETWEEN A PLANT THAT SIMPLY EXISTS AND SEEMS TO 'STAND STILL', AND ONE THAT LOOKS HEALTHY AND VIGOROUS AND REALLY FLOURISHES. MODERN FERTILIZERS HAVE MADE FEEDING REALLY EASY, AND NOW IT ISN'T EVEN A CHORE THAT YOU HAVE TO REMEMBER ON A REGULAR BASIS.

Houseplants are handicapped simply by being contained in a pot. The volume of soil or compost that the roots can explore is strictly limited, and sometimes we expect the same compost to support a large plant for many years.

With a few exceptions, your plants will look better if you feed them. You can buy special fertilizers for flowering plants, foliage plants and even special groups such as saintpaulias, but if you want to keep things simple and use one type of feed for all your plants they will still respond better than if they hadn't been fed at all.

When to feed
If in doubt about a particular plant, check the label or look it up in a book. As a general rule, however, plants should be fed only when they are growing actively and when light and temperature are such that they can actually take advantage of the additional nutrients. This generally means between mid-spring and mid-autumn, but there are exceptions – notably with winter-flowering plants.

Cyclamen are fed during the winter as well as before, and the winter- and spring-flowering forest cacti are fed during the winter but rested in summer. The rule of 'active growth' is more important than the time of year.

Controlled-release fertilizers (see top right) are useful for houseplants, but bear in mind that they are influenced by temperature, so they won't stop releasing nutrients in winter as they would outdoors.

How often to apply
Some trial and error is inevitable. Books and plant labels often give advice like 'feed once a fortnight' or 'feed weekly', but with so many different formulations available such advice may be inappropriate. It assumes a typical liquid houseplant feed. Do not follow this advice too closely if you use one of the other types.

Controlled- and slow-release fertilizers
These are widely used commercially, especially for outdoor container-grown plants, and also for pot plants to keep them healthy until sale. Unlike ordinary fertilizers, the nutrients are released slowly over a period of months, so a couple of applications in a year is all that most plants require.

Controlled-release fertilizers are most useful for outdoor plants because they release the nutrients only when the soil temperature is high enough for the plants to make use of them.

Slow-release fertilizers are most useful for houseplants as a compost (potting soil) additive when potting up an established plant.

Why feed?
These two *Rhoicissus rhomboidea* are the same age and were the same size when bought. The plant on the left has been fed regularly and repotted once; the one on the right has not been fed and shows typical signs of starvation.

Slow-release fertilizers

Slow-release fertilizers are worth adding to the compost (potting soil) because they sustain the plants over a period of perhaps six months. The nutrients in many peat-based (peat-moss based) or peat-substitute composts may become depleted within weeks or perhaps a couple of months.

Liquid feeds

Liquid fertilizers are quick-acting, and useful when a plant needs an immediate boost. Strengths and dilutions vary, so *always follow the manufacturer's advice* for rate and frequency of application. Some are weak and designed to be used at almost every watering, others are very strong and should be applied less frequently.

Pellets and sticks

There are various products designed to take the chore out of regular feeding. These will save you a lot of time and trouble in comparison with liquid feeds, although they may work out more expensive in the long run. Some

DON'T OVER-FEED

❧ Because some feeding is good does not mean that more feeding is better. Do not apply more than the manufacturer recommends, otherwise you might kill your plants. Salts build up in the compost (potting soil) and can affect the intake of water and nutrients which, coupled with an over-stimulation of the plant, can end in collapse.

Fertilizer sticks and pellets

Pot-plant fertilizers are also available in sticks (top) and pellets (above) that you push into the compost (potting soil). Many people find these more convenient to use than having to mix and apply liquid feeds.

are tablet-shaped, others stick-shaped, but the principle is always the same: you make a hole in the compost (potting soil), push in the fertilizer stick or pellet, then leave it to release its nutrients slowly over a period of a month or so (check the instructions).

Slow-release sachets

Slow-release fertilizers are available in sachets that you place inside the pot at the bottom. These are most appropriate when repotting.

Soluble powders

These work on the same principle as liquid feeds, but you simply dissolve the powder in water at the appropriate rate. They often work out less expensive than ordinary liquid fertilizers.

Granular fertilizer

If you have to add a granular or powder fertilizer to the compost (potting soil), use a fork to stir it into the surface, then water it in thoroughly.

Benefits of feeding

To appreciate the benefits of feeding try starting with two plants of the same age and size, then feed just one of the plants regularly. The two *Pilea cadierei* (top) are the plants as bought. The same plants (above) show the effect a couple of months later after the one on the right was given just one dose of slow-release fertilizer.

Choosing a compost

YOUR PLANTS WILL ONLY BE AS GOOD AS THE COMPOST THEY GROW IN. FEEDING WILL HELP TO OVERCOME NUTRITIONAL DEFICIENCIES, BUT THE STRUCTURE OF THE COMPOST IS ALSO IMPORTANT IF THE ROOTS ARE TO GET THE RIGHT BALANCE BETWEEN MOISTURE AND AIR, SO VITAL FOR HEALTHY GROWTH. COMMERCIALLY, COMPOSTS ARE CHOSEN THAT MAKE CAPILLARY WATERING EASY, AND THAT ARE LIGHT TO TRANSPORT, BUT IN THE HOME THEY MAY NOT BE THE MOST APPROPRIATE GROWING MEDIUM.

Compost (potting soil) does more than simply anchor the plant. It also acts as a reservoir for nutrients and, if the structure is right, it achieves the right balance between moisture and air. A good compost also acts as a host to many beneficial micro-organisms.

Earlier generations of gardeners used to formulate their own special potting mixtures for different types of plant. Nowadays, however, composts are available that suit the majority of plants, and only a few types have any special requirements.

The main choice is between loam-based composts and those based on peat (peat moss) or a peat substitute. Most plants will grow well in either type, but there are pros and cons that may make one more or less appropriate for a particular plant.

Loam-based composts
This type of compost uses sterilized loam as its main ingredient, with added sand and peat to improve the structure, as well as fertilizers to supplement the nutrients already present in the loam.

Loam composts have weight, which is a useful attribute for a large plant with a lot of top growth, such as a big palm, since the weight provides stability to the pot.

Peat-based composts
These are light and pleasant to handle, and many plants thrive in them. Sand or other materials are sometimes added, but all of them depend on the addition of fertilizers to support plant growth. Often the fertilizers present in the compost run out quickly, and the plants will almost certainly suffer unless you begin supplementary feeding as soon as the plants show signs of poor growth.

Peat composts are very easy to manage on a commercial scale, with automatic watering systems, but in the home they demand more careful watering than loam composts. They can dry out more completely and become difficult to re-wet, and they are also more easily overwatered.

Some gardeners are reluctant to use peat-based composts on the grounds of depleting wetland areas where peat is excavated. For that reason many alternative products are now being introduced, including composts based on coir (waste from coconuts) and finely pulverized bark. Some use a mixture of materials. Results from these alternative composts can be very variable, depending on the make and formulation. Try a number of plants in several different makes – potting up the same types of plants in each – then decide which is best.

SPECIAL MEDIUMS

A few plants have particular needs that make a general-purpose compost (potting soil) inappropriate. Lime-hating plants, such as azaleas, many begonias, ericas and saintpaulias, are the most common group, and they will grow poorly in ordinary composts. Even peat-based (peat-moss) composts are generally alkaline, because they have lime added to make them suitable for the majority of houseplants. For lime-hating plants you need an 'ericaceous' compost widely available at garden centres.

Bromeliads, cacti and orchids are other groups that have special needs, and you can buy specially formulated composts suitable for these from many specialist nurseries and good garden centres.

Perlite

Gravel

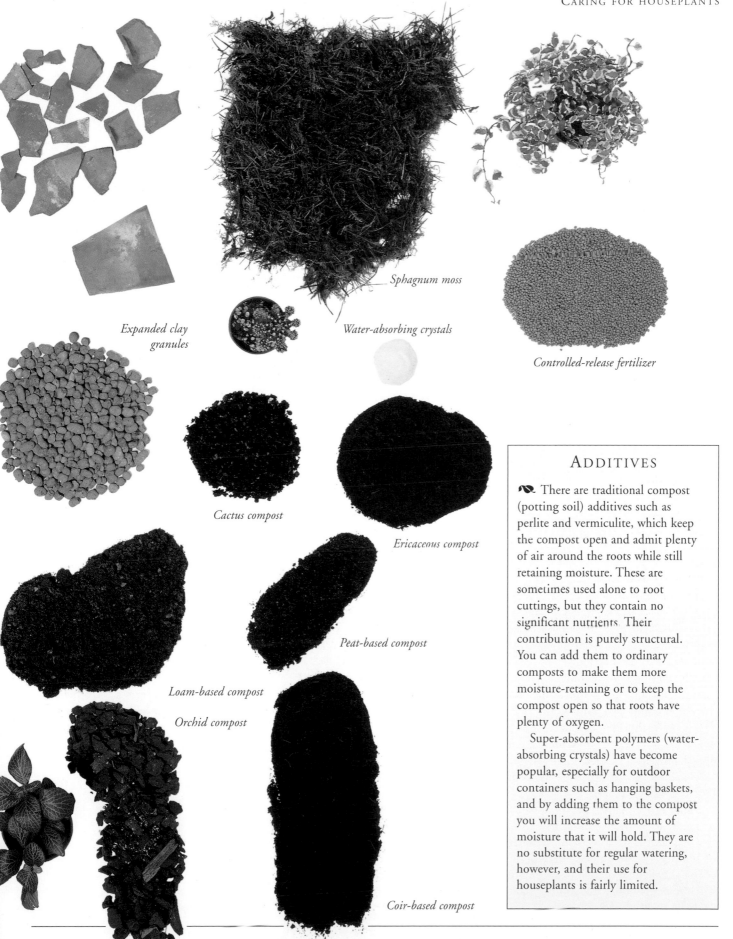

*Expanded clay
granules*

Sphagnum moss

Water-absorbing crystals

Controlled-release fertilizer

Cactus compost

Ericaceous compost

Peat-based compost

Loam-based compost

Orchid compost

Coir-based compost

ADDITIVES

There are traditional compost (potting soil) additives such as perlite and vermiculite, which keep the compost open and admit plenty of air around the roots while still retaining moisture. These are sometimes used alone to root cuttings, but they contain no significant nutrients. Their contribution is purely structural. You can add them to ordinary composts to make them more moisture-retaining or to keep the compost open so that roots have plenty of oxygen.

Super-absorbent polymers (water-absorbing crystals) have become popular, especially for outdoor containers such as hanging baskets, and by adding them to the compost you will increase the amount of moisture that it will hold. They are no substitute for regular watering, however, and their use for houseplants is fairly limited.

Pots and containers

POTS NEEDN'T JUST BE PRACTICAL, THEY CAN BE PRETTY OR INTERESTING TOO. BUT WHATEVER TYPE YOU CHOOSE, THEIR SIZE AND PROPORTION IN RELATION TO THE PLANTS CONTAINED WILL AFFECT HOW THEY ARE PERCEIVED, AND THE POT CAN MAKE OR MAR A PLANT.

Ordinary clay or plastic pots lack visual appeal, and most people hide them in a more decorative cachepot that is slightly larger. If you do this, put gravel, expanded clay granules or a few pebbles in the base to keep the bottom of the pot from contact with the surplus water that collects in the base. Alternatively, pack the space between the inner and outer pots with peat (peat-moss) to absorb most of the moisture, at the same time helping to create a more humid microclimate around the plant. Only use the latter method if you are very methodical about watering and are unlikely to overwater or leave stagnant water sitting at the base of the container. It will be difficult to detect and tip out once the space between the two pots has been filled.

Some plants do look good in clay pots, especially cacti and some succulents. But half-pots are often more appropriate as cacti do not have a large root system, and a shallower pot will usually look more in proportion to the plant. Half-pots have the same diameter as a full pot, but stand only about half the height. Seed pans, which are uncommon now, are similar but shallower; although intended for seed-sowing they can also be used for low or prostrate plants.

Many other plants look better in a half-pot, including azaleas, most begonias, saintpaulias and the majority of bromeliads. Be guided by the type of pot the plant is in when you buy it: if it's a shallow one, use another half-pot when you need to repot.

Some of the better quality plastic pots are coloured and come with a matching saucer, and these can look as attractive as a cache-pot, especially if you choose a colour that is co-ordinated with the room.

You can decorate ordinary clay or plastic pots by painting them freehand or using a stencil. For clay pots use masonry paint (the colours are limited, but you can compensate with a strong design), for plastic pots use acrylic artists' paints.

Square pots are more often used in the greenhouse than indoors, but they are space-saving if you have a collection of small plants such as cacti.

PLASTIC OR CLAY?

The vast majority of the plants on sale are grown in plastic pots: evidence that commercial growers find them satisfactory. Plastic pots are clean, light, easy to handle, remain largely free of algae and are inexpensive. They retain moisture better and the compost (potting soil) is less likely to dry out.

Perhaps surprisingly, clay pots will usually last longer than plastic ones. Plastic pots become brittle with age and even a slight knock is sometimes sufficient to break them. A clay pot won't break unless you actually drop it onto a hard surface. The extra weight of a clay pot will also be of benefit if a plant is large and rather top-heavy.

ABOVE: *This zinc container creates just the right atmosphere for an old-fashioned kitchen setting. If a container is large enough, try using a couple of compatible plants, like the adiantum and pellaea ferns used here.*

ABOVE: *Rush baskets can be very effective for small spring bulbs or compact plants like saintpaulias. Always line them or use them simply as a cache-pot.*

ABOVE: *Ceramic pots look stylish, and so much more colourful than an ordinary clay or plastic pot.*

ABOVE: *Bark baskets look good for houseplants that you would normally associate with trees, such as an ivy.*

ABOVE: *In a modern setting you may want a stylish type of container, like this small zinc one. The purple gynura does not detract from the container, which is a feature in its own right.*

ABOVE: *Terracotta hanging pots look more attractive than the plastic versions for a semi-cascading plant like this nephrolepis fern.*

ABOVE: *This china cache-pot picks up the colour of the cyclamen flowers to create a co-ordinated look.*

ABOVE: *Moss baskets make a nice setting for a few spring plants like primroses, and crocuses. Do not plant directly into this type of container unless you can ensure the surface is protected from drips.*

ABOVE: *Keep an eye open for the unlikely or unexpected. This distinctive container is made from dried fungi! The plant in it is a variegated* Ficus pumila.

ABOVE: *Stoneware pots are appropriate for plants in a kitchen. This one has been planted with* Helxine soleirolii *(syn.* Soleirolia soleirolii*), which reflects the rounded shape of the pot.*

ABOVE: *Terracotta wall planters can be used indoors as well as out. This* Philodendron scandens *will have to be trimmed after a few months to retain the container as a feature.*

ABOVE: *This metal planter is the kind of container that would look stunning in the right setting. You can line it with moss, rather like a hanging basket.*

ABOVE: *Sometimes old hand-made clay pots can be used effectively. The white deposit that often appears on old pots adds to the impression of age. These have been planted with ivies.*

ABOVE: *Matching drip trays are useful, and this one is particularly attractive because it takes three ceramic pots.*

ABOVE: *All kinds of decorative cache-pots are available in stores and garden centres, so it should be easy to choose those that appeal to your own tastes.*

Potting plants

SOONER OR LATER MOST PLANTS NEED REPOTTING, AND IT CAN GIVE AN AILING PLANT A NEW LEASE OF LIFE. BUT NOT ALL PLANTS RESPOND WELL TO FREQUENT REPOTTING, AND SOME PREFER TO BE IN SMALL POTS. KNOWING WHEN TO REPOT, AND INTO WHICH SIZED POT, IS A SKILL THAT DEVELOPS WITH EXPERIENCE.

Never be in too much of a hurry to pot on a plant into a larger container. Plants do not appreciate having their roots disturbed, and any damage to them will result in some check to growth.

Repotting should never simply be an annual routine. It's a job to be thought about annually, but not actually done unless the plant needs it.

Young plants require potting on much more frequently than older ones. Once a large specimen is in a big pot it may be better to keep it growing by repotting into another pot of the same size, by topdressing, or simply by additional feeding.

When repotting is necessary
The sight of roots growing through the base of the pot is not in it itself a sign that repotting is necessary. If the plants have been watered through a capillary mat, or the pot has been placed in a cache-pot, some roots will inevitably grow through the base to seek the water.

If in doubt, knock the plant out of its pot. To remove the root-ball easily, invert the pot and knock the rim on a hard surface while supporting the plant and compost (potting soil) with your hand. It is normal for a few roots to run around the inside of the pot, but if there is also a solid mass of roots it's time to pot on.

There are several ways to repot a plant, but the two described here are among the best.

Pot-in-pot method

1. Prepare the new pot as described in the *Traditional method,* if using a clay pot. However, don't cover the drainage hole at all if using a plastic pot and you intend using a capillary watering mat.

When to repot

A mass of thick roots growing through the bottom of the pot (top) is an indication that it's time to move the plant into a large one. Equally, a mass of roots curled around the edge of the pot (above) is another sign that it's time for a larger container.

POTTING ON, POTTING UP, REPOTTING

Although some of these terms are commonly used interchangeably, their true meanings are specific:

Potting up is what happens the first time a seedling or cutting is given its own pot.

Potting on is the action of replanting the root-ball in a larger pot.

Repotting is sometimes taken to mean replacing the plant in a pot of the same size, but with most of the compost replaced. This is only necessary if the plant cannot be moved into a larger pot.

2. Place a little dampened compost (potting soil) over the base material then insert the existing pot (or an empty one the same size), ensuring that the level of the soil surface will be about 1cm (½in) below the top of the new pot when filled.

3. Pack more compost firmly between the inner and outer pots, pressing it down gently with your fingers. This creates a mould when the inner pot is removed.

4. Remove the inner pot, then take the plant from its original container and drop it into the hole formed in the centre of the new compost. Gently firm the compost around the root-ball, and water thoroughly.

Traditional method

1. Prepare a pot that is one or two sizes larger than the original and, if the pot is a clay one, cover the drainage hole with a piece of broken pot or a few pieces of chipped bark.

2. Make sure that the plant has been watered a short time beforehand, and knock the root-ball out of the old pot. Sometimes you can remove it by pulling gently on the plant, otherwise invert the pot and tap the rim on a hard surface.

3. Place a small amount of compost (potting soil) in the base of the new pot, then position the root-ball so that it is at the right height. If too low or too high, adjust the amount of compost in the base.

4. Trickle more compost around the sides, turning the pot as you work. It's a good idea to use the same kind of compost – peat- (peat-moss) or loam-based – as used in the original pot.

5. Gently firm the compost with the fingers. Make sure there is a gap of about 1–2.5cm (½–1in) between the top of the compost and the rim of the pot, to allow space for watering. Water thoroughly.

TOPDRESSING

❧ Once plants are in large pots, perhaps 25–30cm (10–12in) in diameter, continual potting on into a larger pot may not be practical. Try removing the top few centimetres (inches) of compost (potting soil), loosening it first with a small hand fork. Replace this with fresh potting compost of the same type. This, plus regular feeding, will enable most plants to be grown in the same pot for many years.

Pruning and grooming

GROOMING YOUR PLANTS OCCASIONALLY NOT ONLY KEEPS THEM LOOKING

GOOD, IT ALSO ENABLES YOU TO CHECK THEM FOR EARLY SIGNS OF PESTS AND

DISEASES BEFORE THESE BECOME A PROBLEM.

Some pruning and grooming tasks simply keep the plants looking fresh and tidy, others actually improve them by encouraging bushier growth or promoting further flowering.

Apart from picking off dead flowers, which is best done whenever you notice them, grooming is only a once-a-week task. Most jobs need doing less frequently than this, but by making a routine of tidying up your plants you will almost certainly detect pest, disease and nutritional problems that much earlier. One also learns to appreciate the plants more by close examination, so you will benefit as well as the plants.

Deadheading

This keeps the plant looking tidy, and in many cases encourages the production of more flowers. It also discourages diseases: fungus infections often start on dead or dying flowers, before spreading to the leaves.

Plants with masses of small flowers, such as fibrous-rooted begonias (*B. semperflorens*) are difficult to deadhead often enough, but unless you make some effort the flowers that fall often make a mess of the furniture or sill that they fall on, as well as spoiling the appearance of the plant itself.

Apart from where the flowers appear in a spike, remove the flower stalks as well as the flowers. Sometimes the stalks are most easily removed by hand, using a pulling and twisting motion at the same time.

If the flowers appear in spikes or large heads, such as a hydrangea, cut the whole head or spike back to just above a pair of leaves when the last blooms have finished.

Leaves

Dust and dirt accumulate on leaves as well as on furniture, but this is not always obvious unless the foliage is naturally glossy. This accumulation not only implies neglect, it also harms the plant slightly by cutting down on the amount of light falling on the leaf and thereby hindering photosynthesis, the process by which the plant produces energy for growth.

Wipe smooth leaves with a soft, damp cloth. Some people add a little milk to the water to produce a shine on glossy foliage. The alternative is to use a commercial leaf shine. Some leaf cleaners come as aerosols or sprays, others as impregnated wipes. If you are using an aerosol, follow the manufacturer's instructions carefully and pay particular attention to the recommended spraying distance.

Cloths and sprays are no use for cleaning hairy leaves. Instead, use a small paintbrush as a duster. You can dust cacti in the same way.

Removing leaves
Sooner or later all plants have a few dead leaves. Even evergreens drop old leaves from time to time. Don't let them spoil the appearance of the plant; most are easily removed with a gentle tug, but tough ones may have to be cut off.

TOOLS FOR THE JOB

❧ Most of the equipment you need in order to care for houseplants you will probably already have around the home. You might want to try commercial leaf shines or buy secateurs (floral scissors), but a sponge or soft cloth and kitchen scissors will usually do the job just as well.

It is worth keeping a small grooming kit handy, perhaps in a small box that you can carry around during grooming sessions. It should contain:

❧ Sharp, pointed scissors, or a small pair of secateurs or flower-gathering scissors.

❧ A supply of split canes for supports.

❧ A ball of soft garden string, preferably green, or metal split rings. For some jobs, a reel of green plastic-covered wire is useful.

❧ A sponge for wiping glossy leaves.

❧ A small paintbrush for cleaning hairy leaves.

Leaf wipes
You might find commercial leaf wipes more convenient to use. They leave large, glossy leaves looking shiny and bright.

Deadheading
Removing dead flowers will keep the plant looking smart, and reduce the chance of dead petals encouraging the growth of moulds and other diseases. Some plants also make a mess of the table or windowsill if the flowers are simply allowed to drop.

Immersing foliage
If the plant is small enough to handle conveniently, try swishing the foliage in a bowl of tepid water. Do not do this if the plant has hairy or delicate leaves.

Compact non-flowering plants that don't have hairy leaves – aglaonemas for example – can be cleaned by swishing the foliage in a bowl of tepid water. But make sure that the plant dries off out of direct sunlight, otherwise the leaves may be scorched.

Shaping and training
You can improve the shape of many houseplants by pinching out the growing tips to prevent them from becoming tall and leggy. Removing the tips of the shoots makes the plant bushier. Impatiens, hypoestes, pileas and tradescantias are among the many plants that benefit from this treatment. Start when the plants are young, and repeat it whenever the growth looks too thin and long. This is especially useful for trailers such as tradescantias: a dense, bushy cascade about 30cm (1 ft) long will look much better than thin, weedy-looking shoots of twice the length.

If any all-green shoots develop on a variegated plant, pinch or prune them back to the point of origin.

Climbers and trailers need regular attention. Tie in any new shoots to the support, and cut off any long shoots that spoil the shape.

Sponging
Glossy-leaved plants like this ficus will look smarter if you wipe over the foliage with slightly soapy water occasionally. The plants look healthier and also benefit because dust can reduce the amount of light received and also clog some of the pores through which the plant 'breathes'.

Brushing leaves
Plants with hairy leaves, like this saintpaulia, should not be sponged or cleaned with a leaf wipe. Instead, brush them occasionally with a soft paintbrush.

Pinching out
If you want a bushy rather than a tall or sprawling plant, pinch out the growing tips a few times while it is still young. This will stimulate the growth of sideshoots that will produce a bushier effect. Most plants will respond to this treatment, but beware of doing it to slow-growing plants.

SIMPLE MULTIPLICATION

A plant that you have raised yourself, from seed or a cutting, always seems more special than one that you have bought. Propagation is one of the most deeply satisfying aspects of gardening, and once you have enough plants for your own needs you will still have plenty to exchange with friends.

Growing from seed

IT CAN BE PARTICULARLY GRATIFYING TO TELL ADMIRING FRIENDS THAT

YOU RAISED YOUR ABUTILON OR VENUS FLY TRAP FROM SEED, BUT PEREN-

NIALS CAN BE QUITE A CHALLENGE AND, IN THE CASE OF MIXTURES, NOT

ALL THE PLANTS WILL BE AS GOOD AS NAMED VARIETIES. ANNUALS, ON THE

OTHER HAND, ARE VERY EASY TO GROW AND SELDOM DISAPPOINT.

If you haven't grown houseplants from seed before, start with easy annuals, which will bring quick and reliable results. This spurs most people to try the trickier or more interesting plants like cacti, cycads and ferns (which are actually grown from spores and not true seeds), as well as favourites like saintpaulias.

As a general rule, those houseplants offered by seed merchants that normally deal in the more common and 'everyday' plants are likely to be the

How to sow in a tray

1. Fill the tray loosely with a seed compost (medium) – loam- and peat-based (peat-moss based) are equally satisfactory for the majority of seeds. Do not use a potting compost as the higher level of nutrients these contain can inhibit germination.

2. Level off the compost, using a piece of wood or rigid cardboard, then firm it gently with a 'presser' or piece of wood that will fit within the tray. Make sure that the compost is still level.

3. Sprinkle the seeds as carefully and as evenly as possible over the surface. A good way to do this with small seeds is in a folded piece of paper that you tap gently with a finger as you move it over the surface.

4. Unless the seed is very fine, or the packet says that the seeds should be left exposed to light, sprinkle a little more compost over the top of the seeds. As a guide, cover with a layer of compost that is about the thickness of the seeds themselves. Use an old kitchen sieve to sift the compost over. This keeps back large pieces and makes it easier to spread evenly.

5. Water carefully, using a watering-can fitted with a very fine rose (fine-mist head) – take the tray outdoors to do this. Otherwise stand it in a bowl of water as described for pots opposite. Place the tray in a propagator, or cover it with a sheet of glass. Follow the instructions on the seed packet regarding the required level of light or darkness, and temperature.

SOWING VERY FINE SEED

🕭 Some seeds are very tiny, almost like dust, making them difficult to sow evenly. Mix seed that is this small with a little silver sand in the palm of one hand, then use the finger and thumb of the other to sprinkle the mixture over the surface of your seed tray. If the seed and sand have been well combined, distribution of the seed should be even, especially as the sand will help you judge how evenly you are sowing the seed.

easiest to grow. Those offered by seed merchants specializing in the uncommon or unusual are often more difficult to germinate, but the very fact that they are demanding explains part of their appeal to many enthusiasts.

Many perennial houseplants can be slow to germinate and they may take a couple of years to reach a respectable size. If you have a heated greenhouse or conservatory it makes sense to grow them on in there until they are large enough to be used for indoor display.

Sow in trays if you need a lot of plants, otherwise use pots, as these take up less space.

Pricking out

As soon as the seedlings are large enough to handle, prick them out, either into individual pots or into seed trays, to grow on until large enough for their own pots.

Use a potting compost (medium) for this, and always lift the seedlings carefully by their leaves rather than by the fragile stem.

AVOID THE CONDENSATION PROBLEM

Condensation will form inside a propagator or on the sheet of glass covering the tray or pot. If this is so heavy that drips start to fall on the germinating seedlings, ventilate the propagator or wipe the glass.

How to sow in a pot

1. Fill the pot with a seed compost (medium), but this time use a round presser to firm and level it gently. Make a presser from wood, or simply use a jam-jar.

3. Water by the immersion method. Stand the pot in a bowl of water, making sure that the water level remains below the top of the compost. Remove the pot to drain once the surface of the compost has become moist. Using this method, even the smallest seeds will not be disturbed.

2. Sow the seeds as evenly as possible. The easiest way to sow over the small area of a pot is to sprinkle the seeds between finger and thumb, as you might sprinkle salt. Sprinkle more compost over the sown seeds unless they are very fine, or the instructions on the packet advise otherwise. Most seeds should be covered with approximately their own depth of compost.

4. Place in a propagator or cover with a sheet of glass.

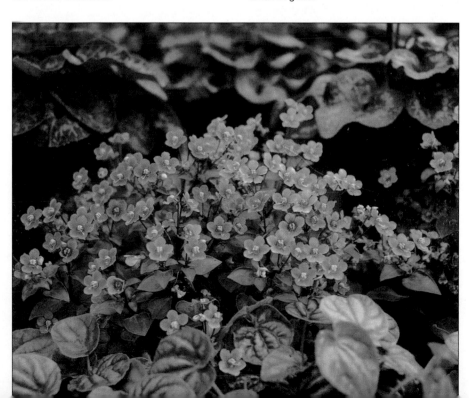

RIGHT: **Exacum affine** *is one of the easiest houseplants to try raising from seed. Sow in spring to flower in summer and autumn, or in autumn to flower the following spring.*

Stem cuttings

MOST HOUSEPLANTS CAN BE RAISED FROM STEM CUTTINGS, AND SOME ARE SO

EASY THAT THEY WILL EVEN ROOT IN WATER. OTHERS ARE MORE CHALLENG-

ING, REQUIRING ROOTING HORMONES AND A PROPAGATOR.

Impatiens

Impatiens are often grown from seed, but they root readily from softwood cuttings.

As old plants often lose their compact shape, take a few cuttings periodically.

Geraniums

Geranium (pelargonium) softwood cuttings root readily. You can use this technique for

zonal geraniums, regal geraniums like these, and scented-leaved geraniums.

Most houseplants can be propagated from softwood cuttings taken in spring, and many of the shrubby plants root from semi-ripe cuttings taken later in the year.

Softwood cuttings

This method of taking cuttings is similar to semi-ripe cuttings, but choose the ends of new shoots. Take softwood cuttings after the first flush of spring but before the shoots have become hard. Now follow the same procedure as for semi-ripe cuttings.

Cuttings in water

Softwood cuttings can often be rooted in water, especially easy ones like coleus and impatiens.

Almost fill a jam-jar with water and fold a piece of wire-netting (chicken wire) over the top, or use a piece of aluminium foil with holes pierced in it. Take the cuttings in the normal way but, instead of inserting them into compost (potting soil), rest them on the netting or foil, with the end of the stem in water.

Top up the water as necessary. When roots have formed, pot the cuttings up into individual pots using a sandy potting compost. Keep the plants out of direct sunlight for at least a week to give them a chance to become established in the pot.

HORMONES HELP ROOTING

Some plants, such as impatiens and some tradescantias, root readily even without help from a rooting hormone. Others, and especially semi-ripe cuttings, will benefit from the use of a rooting hormone. Rooting hormones are available as powders or liquids, and their use usually results in more rapid rooting and, in the case of the trickier kinds of plants, a higher success rate.

How to take semi-ripe cuttings

1. Fill a pot with a cuttings compost (medium) or use a seed compost, and firm it to remove large pockets of air.

2. Make the cuttings 10–15cm (4–6in) long (they may have to be shorter on very compact plants), choosing the current season's growth after the first flush of growth but before the whole shoot has become hard. They should be firm yet flexible, and offer some resistance when bent.

3. Trim the cutting just below a leaf joint, using a sharp knife, and remove the lower leaves to produce a clear stem to insert into the compost.

4. Dip the cut end of the cutting into a rooting hormone. If using a powder, moisten the end in water first so that it adheres.

5. Make a hole in the compost with a small dibber or a pencil, and insert the cutting so that the bottom leaves are just above the compost. Firm the compost gently around the stem to remove large air pockets. You can usually insert several cuttings around the edge of a pot.

6. Water the cuttings (adding a fungicide to the water will help to reduce the risk of the cuttings rotting), then label and place in a propagator. If you don't have a propagator, cover the pot with a clear plastic bag, making sure it does not touch the leaves. Keep in a light place, but *out of direct sunlight*.

If a lot of condensation forms, reverse the bag or ventilate the propagator until excess condensation ceases to form. Do not allow the compost to dry out.

Pot up the cuttings individually once they have formed a good root system.

Leaf cuttings

LEAF CUTTINGS ALWAYS SEEM MORE FASCINATING TO ROOT THAN STEM CUTTINGS, AND THERE ARE PLENTY OF HOUSEPLANTS THAT YOU CAN PROPAGATE THIS WAY. THE TECHNIQUES ARE EASY AS WELL AS FUN, AND SOME OF THE MOST POPULAR PLANTS, SUCH AS SAINTPAULIAS, FOLIAGE BEGONIAS, STREPTOCARPUS AND SANSEVIERIAS, CAN BE RAISED FROM LEAF CUTTINGS.

Square leaf cuttings

1. First cut the leaf into strips about 3cm (1¼in) wide, in the general direction of the main veins, using a sharp knife or razor-blade.

There are several types of leaf cuttings described here. For leaf petiole cuttings you need to remove the leaves with a length of stalk attached. Some leaves form new plants from the leaf blades, especially from points where the veins have been injured. For square leaf cuttings, instead of placing a whole leaf on the compost (medium), you can cut it into squares and insert these individually. With leaf midrib cuttings, the long, narrow leaves of plants such as streptocarpus can simply be sliced into sections and treated like square leaf cuttings.

Leaf petiole cuttings

1. Use only healthy leaves that are mature but not old. Remove the leaf with about 5cm (2in) of stalk, using a sharp knife or razorblade.

2. Fill a tray or pot with a suitable rooting compost (medium), then make a hole with a dibber or pencil.

PLANTS TO GROW FROM LEAF CUTTINGS

🍃 Leaf petiole cuttings
Begonias (other than *B. rex*)
Peperomia caperata
Peperomia metallica
Saintpaulia

🍃 Leaf blade cuttings
Begonia rex

🍃 Leaf midrib cuttings
Gesneria
Sansevieria*
Sinningia speciosa (gloxinia)
Streptocarpus

* If you use this method for the variegated *S. trifasciata* 'Laurentii' the plantlets will not be variegated.

3. Insert the stalk into the hole, angling the cutting slightly, then press the compost gently around the stalk to firm it in. The base of the blade of the leaf should sit on the surface of the compost. You should be able to accommodate a number of cuttings in a seed tray or large pot. Water well, preferably with a fungicide, and allow surplus moisture to drain.

4. Place the cuttings in a propagator, or cover with a clear plastic bag. Make sure that the leaves do not touch the glass or plastic, and remove condensation periodically.

Keep the cuttings warm and moist, in a light place out of direct sunlight. Young plants usually develop within a month or two, but leave them until they are large enough to be handled easily.

2. Next cut across the strips to form small squares of leaf.

3. Fill a tray with a rooting compost (medium), then insert the squares on edge, making sure that the edge that was nearest to the leaf stalk faces downwards.

4. After a month or two you should have plenty of young plants that have grown from the leaf squares. Once these are well established, pot them up individually

Leaf midrib cuttings

1. Remove a healthy, undamaged leaf from the parent plant, ideally one that has only recently fully expanded.

2. Place the leaf face down on a firm, clean surface, such as a sheet of glass. Cut the leaf into strips, no wider than 5cm (2in).

LONGITUDINAL LEAF CUTTINGS

❧ An alternative method of propagating streptocarpus:

❧ Lay the leaf on a hard surface, and cut it twice along the length of the leaf, on both sides of the main vein. Discard the main vein.

❧ Insert these halves into the compost, so that they stand on edge with about one-third in the compost.

3. Fill a tray or large pot with a rooting compost (medium), and insert the cuttings into this about 2.5cm (1in) apart. Insert the end that was nearest the stalk into the compost. About one-third of the cutting should be in the compost.

Young plants will eventually appear from the compost. Pot these up individually when they are large enough to handle safely.

Leaf blade cuttings

1. Select a healthy leaf, and sever it close to the base of the main stalk.

2. Cut off the attached stalk close to the blade.

3. Cut across the main and secondary veins on the underside of the leaf, using a sharp knife or razor-blade. Make the cuts about 2.5cm (1in) apart.

4. Fill a seed tray with a rooting compost (medium), then peg the leaf so that the back is in contact with the compost. Make several small U-shaped 'staples' from pieces of galvanized wire, to act as anchors.

5. Alternatively, instead of using wire staples, you can hold the leaf in contact with the compost by using small stones as weights.

6. Keep in a propagator, or in a warm place, in a light position but out of direct sunlight. Do not allow the compost to become dry.

New plants will eventually grow, and once these look well established, pot them up individually. Often the old leaf has disintegrated by this time, but if not, just cut the new plants free of the old leaf.

LEFT: **Begonia rex** *should be propagated using leaf-blade cuttings, rather than other methods.*

Easy division

DIVISION IS THE QUICKEST AND EASIEST OF ALL METHODS OF PROPAGATION.
THE RESULTS ARE INSTANT, AND MOST PLANTS WITH A CROWN OR THAT
FORM A CLUMP CAN BE PROPAGATED THIS WAY.

Many ferns can be divided, including adiantum, phyllitis, and *Pteris cretica*. Marantas, and related genera such as calathea, also form a clump and lend themselves to division. Other popular houseplants to try are anthuriums and aspidistras.

Water the plant about an hour before you divide it. If the roots are thick and fleshy, have a sharp knife handy to cut though them.

Dividing a plant

1. Knock the plant out of its pot. If the plant is large and the pot full of roots, you may need to invert the pot and tap the rim on a hard surface. Place a hand over the root-ball to catch it as it falls free.

2. Pull away some of the compost (potting soil) from the bottom and sides, freeing some of the roots in the process.

3. Try pulling the plant apart with your hands, first into two pieces, and then into smaller ones if you need a lot of new plants.

4. Sometimes the tough or fleshy roots make this difficult: chlorophytums are an example. If this is the case, prise the roots apart with a hand fork and separate the clump into smaller pieces with a sharp knife.

5. Replant healthy young pieces of the root clump, using a smaller pot and a good potting compost (medium). It may be necessary to trim back some of the largest roots with a knife, but try to leave the small, fibrous ones intact.

After watering, keep the plants in good light but out of direct sun, at least until they have become established and started to grow again.

Layering

LAYERING IS A USEFUL TECHNIQUE IF YOU REQUIRE JUST A FEW EXTRA OR REPLACEMENT PLANTS. ORDINARY LAYERING IS ONLY PRACTICAL FOR A FEW PLANTS INDOORS, BUT AIR LAYERING IS A POPULAR WAY TO IMPROVE AN OLD FICUS THAT HAS BECOME BARE AT THE BASE.

Ordinary layering is most appropriate for climbers or trailers with long and flexible shoots that can easily be pegged down into pots close to the parent plant. Ivies and *Philodendron scandens* are plants that readily lend themselves to this form of propagation.

Air layering is most often used for large ficus, such as *F. elastica*, but the method can also be used for other plants, such as dracaenas. Normally plants are air layered on an area of bare stem just below the leafy part, but if a few old leaves are in the way cut these off flush with the stem.

Ordinary layering

1. Fill a few small pots with a seed or cuttings compost (medium), and position them close to the parent plant.

2. Choose long, healthy shoots with young growth, and untangle them from the rest of the plant so that they can be pegged down into the pots.

3. Use pieces of bent wire to hold the stem in contact with the compost where there is a leaf joint. It does not matter if the stem is slightly covered by the compost.

4. When the roots have formed – usually after about four weeks – and new shoots begin to grow, sever the new plant from its parent. Keep the newly severed plant in a light position out of direct sunlight, and pay special attention to watering, until it is well established and obviously growing strongly.

ABOVE: **Philodendron scandens** *is one of the few plants which you can successfully propagate by ordinary layering.*

ABOVE: *Try air layering a leggy* Ficus elastica *'Robusta' and you will once more have a plant like this.*

Air layering

1. Make a sleeve out of a piece of clear plastic and secure it below the point where the layer is to be made, using a plastic-covered twist-tie or adhesive tape. Then, using a sharp knife or blade, make an upward-facing cut about 2.5cm (1in) long, finishing just below a leaf joint. Make sure that you do not cut more than about one-third of the way through the stem, otherwise the top may break.

2. Brush inside the wound with a rooting hormone. A small paintbrush is useful for this. To hold the wound open, insert some moist sphagnum moss into the incision, or use a small piece of matchstick.

3. Pack plenty of moist sphagnum moss around the area, then bring up the plastic sleeve to hold it in place.

4. Secure the top of the sleeve with another twist-tie or some adhesive tape.

5. Check the moss occasionally to make sure that it is still moist, and to see if any roots have formed.

6. Once new roots are visible through the sleeve, cut off the stem just below the root-ball. Loosen the ball of moss slightly, but do not attempt to remove the moss when you pot up the plant. As the root system will still be small at this stage, it may be necessary to provide a stake for a few weeks.

Offsets and plantlets

OFFSETS AND PLANTLETS PROVIDE YOU WITH NEW PLANTS FOR THE MINIMUM

OF EFFORT – AND YOU DON'T HAVE TO SACRIFICE THE PARENT PLANT.

A few plants obligingly grow 'babies' on their leaves – just waiting to root when they come into contact with the compost (potting soil). Others produce plantlets on runners and raising new plants from these is as simple as pegging them down. Many plants – such as bromeliads – produce new shoots clustered around the old ones. These are easily detached and potted up.

Plantlets

Two succulents popularly grown as curiosities carry baby plants on their leaves: *Kalanchoe daigremontiana (syn. Bryophyllum daigremontianum)* and *K. Tubiflora (syn. B. tubiflorum).* The plantlets often fall off and can be found growing in the compost (potting soil) at the base of the parent plant. Just lift these up carefully after loosening the compost, and pot them up individually. Alternatively, remove the largest of the plantlets from the leaves before they fall, and gently press them into the surface of a cuttings compost (medium). Other viviparous plants like this, such as *Asplenium bulbiferum,* can be treated in the same way.

Tolmiea menziesii has young plantlets at the base of its leaves. Just detach a parent leaf, cut off the surplus leaf blade around the plantlet, and bury it just below the compost, with the plantlet still visible.

Runners

Some popular houseplants, such as *Saxifraga stolonifera,* produce plantlets on long runners, others, like *Chlorophytum comosum,* produce them at the ends of arching stems. All of these are very easy to propagate.

Place small pots filled with a cuttings compost (medium) around the parent plant and peg down the plantlets into them using pieces of bent wire or hairpins, to hold them in close contact with the compost. Keep well watered and sever the plantlets from the parent plant once plenty of roots have formed and the new plant has started to grow.

Offsets

Some plants produce offsets – new growth close to the old that can be separated and grown on independently – and this is normal with bromeliads.

Bromeliad offsets

1. Bromeliads produce offsets around the edge of the main flowering part of the plant, which later dies. Pot up these offsets when they are about a third the height of the parent plant.

Runners

1. *Chlorophytum comosum* is easy to propagate from plantlets produced at the ends of long, arching stems.

2. Peg the plantlets down into small pots, using pieces of bent wire to hold them in position.

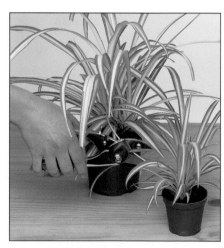

3. Sever the plants from their parent once they have rooted well and are growing strongly.

2. They can usually be pulled away easily, but if necessary cut them away with a knife.

3. Pot the offsets up individually.

4. Firm the plants in, then water and keep in a warm, humid position, out of hot direct sunlight, until they show signs of new growth.

Many epiphytic bromeliads (those that in nature grow in trees or on rocks) have flowering rosettes that die after blooming. Before these plants die, they produce plenty of offsets around the old mature rosette. Leave these on until they are about one-third of the size of the parent plant, then detach them and pot up individually. Most can simply be pulled off by hand, but the tough ones will have to be severed with a sharp knife.

Some terrestrial bromeliads, such as ananas, produce offsets on stolons (short horizontal stems). Remove the plant from its container and cut off the offsets without causing too much damage to the parent.

Pot up the offsets without delay, and keep moist. Position them in good light but out of direct sunlight. They will soon start to grow independently and should then be treated normally.

Propagating from plantlets

1. *Kalanchoe tubiflora* (syn. *Bryophyllum tubiflorum*) produces plenty of plantlets at the ends of its leaves. Remove the plantlets with a gentle tug, and avoid holding the roots.

2. Plant them in a free-draining cuttings compost (medium), where they will soon grow away as young plants.

3. *Kalanchoe daigremontiana* (syn. *Bryophyllum daigremontianum*) produces plantlets around the edges of its leaves. Treat like the previous species, or simply peg down a whole leaf.

4. The ensuing plantlets can be potted up singly when they are larger.

Special techniques

SPECIAL TECHNIQUES LIKE CANE CUTTINGS, LEAF-BUD CUTTINGS, CACTI CUTTINGS AND CACTI GRAFTING ARE USEFUL SKILLS TO ACQUIRE. EVEN IF YOU DON'T USE THE METHODS OFTEN, THEY ARE INVALUABLE FOR PROPAGATING CERTAIN PLANTS.

Some houseplants with thick and erect stems, such as cordylines, dracaenas and dieffenbachias, can be propagated by a technique known as cane cuttings. This is a good method to try if a plant has lost most of its leaves and you are left with a long length of bare stem. In this case, you might as well use the leggy shoots for cane cuttings.

Leaf-bud cuttings are sometimes used for *Ficus elastica,* especially where more plants are required than you could achieve with air layering. You can also use this method of propagation for *Aphelandra squarrosa,* dracaenas, epipremnums, *Monstera deliciosa* and philodendrons.

The majority of cacti will root fairly easily from cuttings, but their odd shapes, as well as their prickles, call for special techniques.

If the cactus has rounded pads (like opuntias), just cut new pads off making a straight cut across the joint. Leave the cutting exposed for about 48 hours for the wound to form a callus. Then insert the cutting into a mixture of grit or coarse sand and peat (peat moss) or peat substitute. Once the cutting has rooted and started to grow, pot it up into a normal cactus compost (medium).

Columnar cacti can often be propagated if the top 5–10cm (2–4in) of stem is removed. Dry off as described above, before inserting the cutting.

Flat-stemmed cacti such as epiphyllums can be cut into lengths about 5cm (2in) long. Dry off as usual then insert upright in the compost.

Cane cuttings

1. Cut the thick stem into pieces about 5–7.5cm (2–3in) long, making sure that each piece has at least one node (the area between two points where leaves were attached).

2. You can insert them vertically, but they are usually laid horizontally with the lower half pressed into the compost. Make sure that the leaf buds are pointing upwards.

Leaf-bud cuttings

1. Select a young stem in spring or summer, and cut it into 1–2.5cm (1/2–1in) sections, each with one leaf and its bud.

BLEEDING WOUNDS

❧ Some succulents, such as euphorbias, produce a milky latex when cut. If this happens, dip the cutting into tepid water for a few seconds to stop the flow. Hold a damp cloth over the cut surface on the parent plant to stop the bleeding. As the sap of some is an irritant, be careful not to get it near your eyes or on your skin.

HANDLING PRICKLY CACTI

❧ Thick gloves make it possible to handle some spiny cacti while taking cuttings, as you do not have to grip the plant hard, but many will simply pierce the gloves. To handle these, fold a newspaper over several times to form a thick band a couple of centimetres (about an inch) wide, then grip the plant with this, holding the 'handles' formed by the ends. A flexible piece of cardboard can be used in a similar way, but be careful not to use anything so hard that the spines are damaged.

Ferns from spores

1. Fill a shallow pot with a peaty compost (peat-moss potting soil). Some people then sprinkle a thin layer of brick dust over the top. Firm it gently so that it is lightly compacted and level.

2. Sprinkle the spores over the surface as evenly as possible.

3. Cover the pot with a piece of glass and stand it in a saucer of water (rain or soft water is best). Keep in a warm, shaded position, and make sure that there is some water in the saucer.

BELOW: *Fern spores are usually sold to amateurs as mixtures of either hardy or tropical species. This* Asplenium nidus *is one fern that a mixture might include, but if you want to propagate a particular species it is worth saving and sowing the spores from your own plants.*

4. In about a month the tiny prothalli will start to grow and gradually cover the surface. It is essential that the compost remains moist at this stage. It is also worth keeping the glass over the pot.

5. A month or two later the ferns proper should begin to appear. At this stage, remove the glass but still keep out of direct hot sunlight. When large enough to handle, prick out the little clumps of ferns into a seed tray.

When the small ferns are large enough to handle easily and a suitable size for their own pot, prick them out into individual pots.

CREATIVE DISPLAYS

Whether you collect houseplants as a philatelist collects stamps, or whether you choose them in the same way as an interior designer selects a painting, you have to find positions that will not only please the plant, but also suit the décor.

Garden rooms and conservatories

WITH A GARDEN ROOM OR CONSERVATORY YOU CAN GROW ALMOST ANY HOUSEPLANT SUCCESSFULLY, AS WELL AS MANY MORE FOR WHICH YOU WOULD NORMALLY NEED A GREENHOUSE. HOWEVER, YOU WILL HAVE TO RESOLVE THE CONFLICT BETWEEN THE NEEDS OF PLANTS AND HUMANS, FOR WHAT IS A COMFORTABLE ENVIRONMENT FOR TROPICAL PLANTS MAY NOT BE COMFORTABLE FOR YOU. WITH CAREFUL PLANNING, HOWEVER, YOU CAN MAKE THE GARDEN ROOM AN EXTENSION OF THE LIVING AREA, WHERE YOU CAN ENJOY HOUSEPLANTS AT THEIR VERY BEST.

Many conservatories and garden rooms are built on as a home extension or a sun room where the garden can be enjoyed when the weather is pleasant but not warm, and in which the plants are merely decorative accessories. You can, however, create a veritable jungle atmosphere, with plants from floor to roof, and hot and humid air to match.

Mainly for people

If a sun room or conservatory is to be a comfortable place to sit for long periods and enjoy the view of the garden, a few attractive chairs, a coffee table and a few elegant pot plants dotted around are all that's required. It just becomes another room.

Paint the back wall white or cream, plant a bougainvillea against it, buy a few big palms and add one or two flowering shrubs such as *Nerium oleander,* and perhaps an orange or lemon in an attractive tub, and you will have a room with instant charm.

Mainly for plants

If your conservatory was bought mainly to increase the number and type of houseplants that you can grow, treat it like a greenhouse. Indeed the distinction between some modern lean-to greenhouses and garden rooms can be a little blurred.

Make the most of climbers; these will clothe the wall and cover the roof space if you secure galvanized wires at about 30–60cm (1–2ft) intervals for support. The roof cover will provide welcome shade in the summer, and if

you choose deciduous climbers such as a grapevine or a passiflora, the other inhabitants will receive full light at the time of year when they most need it. Even so, climbers such as grapes may still need to be cut back periodically during the summer to prevent them from dominating and casting too much shade.

Plant climbers and wall shrubs in the ground if possible, by lifting the paving and making planting pits. Use special display shelves, or improvise your own. Don't just arrange plants around the edge of the structure, create islands of plants, or use them as a backdrop for seats, which can be almost surrounded with plants.

Hanging baskets should thrive, so use plenty of them and be adventurous with what you plant. Although traditional bedding plants can be used in a conservatory, cascading fuchsias or curtains of columneas are usually much more spectacular.

For healthy houseplants, lay a floor that won't come to harm if you splash water about. Use a humidifier if possible, so that the air is aways moist in warm weather, and provide heating for the winter. A minimum of 7°C (45°F) is sufficient to keep most houseplants alive, while the majority of tender types will survive the winter at 13°C (55°F) minimum.

ABOVE: *Bold, tall plants, like this palm, can be used as an eye-catching feature in a conservatory. It also emphasizes the vertical line of the magnificent wrought-iron staircase.*

OPPOSITE: *Citrus fruits, such as oranges, do not do well indoors, but they make excellent conservatory plants. Try painting your conservatory wall white to reflect light and to make an attractive backdrop against which to view your plants.*

TOP RIGHT: *By keeping most of the planting around the edge, and using plenty of hanging baskets, you can give the impression of lush plant growth while still retaining an attractive sitting area.*

ABOVE RIGHT: *Make the most of available space. Plant climbers against the house wall, and use hanging baskets, which will do much better in the improved light than indoors.*

RIGHT: *Plants should thrive in a conservatory, and you can use bold all-green foliage groups like this. With a tiled floor you can provide plenty of moisture and humidity without worrying about drips or splashed water.*

Porch plants

USE YOUR PORCH TO GROW THE TOUGHER HOUSEPLANTS THAT NEED
PLENTY OF SPACE AND GOOD LIGHT. YOU CAN EVEN MAKE IT LOOK LIKE
A SMALL CONSERVATORY.

A porch influences the visitor's first impression of your home, so one that is well clothed with plants rather than bare and bleak will make a warmer welcome. An enclosed porch can be awash with colour the year round, but with an open porch in an exposed or cold position you will have to be content with hardy foliage plants for the cold months.

Enclosed porches
An enclosed porch can be like a mini lean-to greenhouse, and you can enjoy lush foliage and colourful flowers every month of the year. However, try to avoid using plants that will resent the sudden, icy blasts of air that occur when the outer door is opened in cold weather. Intolerant plants will soon drop their leaves and probably die.

Choose mainly plants recommended for cool temperatures, such as primulas, bowls of bulbs such as hyacinths and tulips, or cyclamen and azaleas for the winter. During the summer, regal and zonal geraniums (pelargoniums) do well in the hot atmosphere of such a small enclosed space, and cacti and succulents usually thrive. Provided that the porch can be maintained above freezing temperature, most cacti and succulents will benefit from being left there during the winter. The majority of cacti flower better if they have experienced a cold period during the winter.

Make use of climbers against at least one of the walls: passifloras would do well, but are generally too rampant. Choose something that is more easily restrained, such as *Hoya carnosa* or *Jasminum polyanthum* (be prepared to

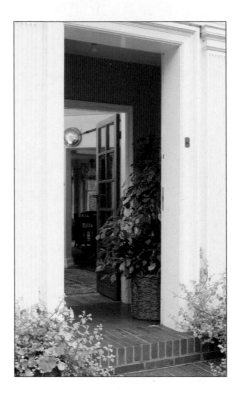

ABOVE: *Porches can be bright or gloomy, protected or exposed. Choose plants appropriate to the conditions. This large* **Ficus benajamina** *will be happy in this position for the summer months, but will have to be brought indoors once the weather turns cold.*

keep it cut back once well established), or even a bougainvillea. Or go for foliage effect with *Cissus antarctica* or *Rhoicissus rhomboidea* (syn. *Cissus rhombifolia*).

If the porch is large, you can use plenty of big plants in floor-standing pots, such as *Fatsia japonica* (a variegated variety will look brighter in a porch), or perhaps an oleander (*Nerium oleander*).

Shelves will be needed to display small plants. If there are no built-in shelves, use the small free-standing display units sold for greenhouses, or special plant stands.

Open porches
Even an open porch can be made attractive. Group plenty of pots of hardy evergreens such as *Aucuba japonica varieties, Fatsia japonica,* skimmias (most have attractive berries in winter), and ivies if you want a trailer or climber. If you have pot-grown camellias and rhododendrons, for example, you can bring them into the porch for extra colour when they are in bloom.

Erica × *hyemalis, E. gracilis, Solanum capsicastrum* and its hybrids, even year-round chrysanthemums, will all provide colour for weeks or even months before having to be discarded.

During the summer, many of the tougher indoor plants can be placed in your porch. Yuccas will do well, and the variegated chlorophytums are reliable, but you can use plants as diverse as the brightly coloured coleus and flowering bougainvilleas. Don't be afraid to add a few unusual hardy foliage plants, such as rhubarb, to create a talking point.

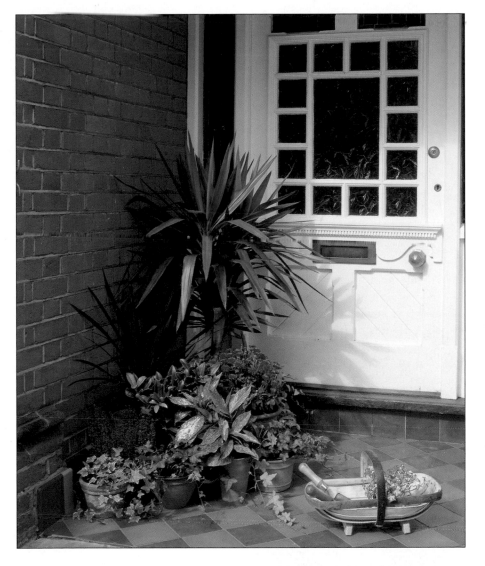

PRACTICAL PROBLEMS

✽ Most houseplants will thrive in an enclosed porch if you avoid extremely high or low temperatures.

✽ A small electric heater coupled to a thermostat will keep it frostproof at little cost, and a fan heater will warm the air rapidly when the door is open. But blasts of cold are hard to avoid, so don't persevere with plants that seem to resent the position.

✽ Too much heat is the main problem in summer. Unlike a greenhouse or conservatory, ventilation is often inadequate. If the porch is in a position where it receives a lot of direct sun, be sure to fit at least one automatic ventilator and, whenever possible, open all the windows before the temperature rises. However, bear in mind that these solutions may affect the security of your property.

✽ Shading will help, and you may find the shade offered by a climber more acceptable than blinds or shading paints.

OPPOSITE: *This large regal pelargonium is kept indoors as a houseplant, but moved to the porch in full flower so that it can be shared with passers-by.*

ABOVE: *This indoor yucca is happy to stand outdoors for the summer in a sheltered position, and it gives height and 'presence' to the rest of the group, which is made up of tough houseplants that will also tolerate cold conditions.*

RIGHT: *The porch is where indoor plants can rub shoulders with hardy plants. Here, a tender begonia has been used with hardy miniature daffodils grown in a pot, and a pot-grown rosemary. The miniature roses were bought as houseplants but will later be planted in the garden. The rhododendron is totally hardy.*

Living-rooms

THE LIVING-ROOM IS THE PLACE WHERE MOST PEOPLE GROW THEIR HOUSE-
PLANTS. IT IS LIKELY TO BE WARM AND LIGHT, WITH PLENTY OF SPACE TO
DISPLAY PLANTS CREATIVELY.

The living-room is probably the best room for houseplants. There are usually large windows – often ceiling to floor patio doors at one end – plenty of standing places such as windowsills, tables and ledges or alcoves, and usually ample space for large floor-standing specimens. It is also the room that most people make an effort to decorate attractively, and where they spend most of their leisure time.

Just as the appearance of a room can be changed by moving the furniture around, so the positioning of plants can radically alter how a room looks. This is especially true for large specimen plants that act as focal points, and for groups of large plants used to screen areas.

In living-rooms, the colour and texture of plants can play important roles, especially the way in which they blend or contrast with the background. Try to use the juxtaposition of contrasting forms, shapes and colours to emphasize the visual impact of the plants.

Colour always needs to be considered. A foliage or flower colour that blends with an accompanying pot or ornament will look tasteful, but the wall behind will look best if it is neutral, or plain and contrasting. But for a special effect you may want to blend the colours of your plants with a more decorative background – perhaps white daisy-like flowers with green ferns, and green-and-white dieffenbachia against white net curtains, all set off on a white table.

Texture adds variety. The long purple hairs of a gynura will be best emphasized by a smooth pale background, a prickly cactus may look more in keeping with the colour and texture of rough bricks behind. The papery, wing-like leaves of caladiums will need a colour behind that brings out the beauty of these exotic-looking leaves (as they vary from white and green to bright red, the best background depends on the variety). But above all, the leaves of caladiums need to be illuminated well, either from behind or in front, to show off their delicate texture. The puckered leaves of the *Begonia masoniana* have a texture that you want to touch, adding tactile to visual stimulation.

Shape will compensate for lack of colour. Most philodendrons have large and interestingly shaped leaves, like the fingered and fringed *P. bipinnatifidum* and the more deeply cut *P. selloum,* and among the large-leaved ficus, *F. lyrata* has enormous, waxy leaves the shape of an upside-down violin. Plants like this will create as much interest as those with bright flowers or brilliant foliage, and they do it in a restrained way that creates the right mood for an elegant and sophisticated living-room.

Making a mini cactus garden

1. Make sure there are adequate drainage holes. Cover these with pieces of broken pot.

2. Although a cactus compost (potting soil) is preferable, you can use an ordinary compost.

3. If you have a very prickly cactus to plant, hold it in a strip of folded paper like this.

LEFT: *Cacti and succulents often look best in small groups, and a half-pot or shallow clay container is particularly appropriate.*

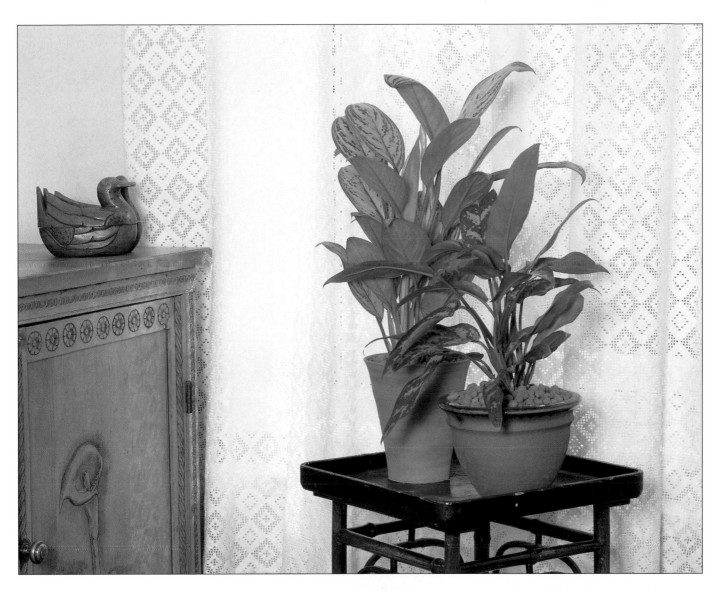

ABOVE: *Living rooms are usually light and spacious. Plants like aglaonemas, which like bright light but not direct sunlight, often do well by a window with net curtains. White net curtains make an excellent backdrop for many plants.*

RIGHT: *The living room is where you might want to use an especially beautiful container as a cache-pot for an appropriately impressive plant, like this azalea. As the blooms on one flowering plant die, replace with another, so that your special corner of the room always looks fresh and colourful.*

FAR RIGHT: *Succulents like this crassula are undemanding provided you can give them a position near the window. As they lack colour, try using a bright pot.*

Kitchens

IN THE DAYS WHEN KITCHENS WERE DARK AND DINGY AND COOKING WAS DONE WITH COAL GAS, OR EVEN AN OPEN RANGE, THE KITCHEN WAS A PLACE FOR ONLY THE TOUGHEST OF PLANTS. MODERN KITCHENS ARE USUALLY LIGHT, BRIGHT AND RELATIVELY SPACIOUS. PLANTS SHOULD THRIVE HERE, AND THERE ARE PLENTY OF OPPORTUNITIES TO USE THEM.

PROBLEM SPOTS

❧ Bear in mind that heat rises, so do not place any plants where the heat from cooking will make life uncomfortable – on shelves or cupboards near the cooker for example.

❧ Few houseplants will be happy with icy blasts from an open back door in winter. If possible, keep your plants well away from the door.

As always, the windowsill is the first place to fill with plants. Here you can grow those that need good light, but if the room receives direct sun at the hottest part of the day you will be restricted to those that tolerate the sun's rays intensified by the glass, such as cacti and succulents, geraniums (pelargoniums) and tradescantias.

Make the most of the tops of cupboards near the window for trailing plants. Although watering can be difficult, and the light near the ceiling will be poor, as the plants trail and tumble they enter the zone of better light and most will thrive. If they become thin and straggly, keep pinching back the long shoots to keep the growth bushy and compact.

Avoid trailing or cascading plants on or near work surfaces or eating areas. Choose plants with upright growth that will not get in the way. *Sansevieria trifasciata* 'Laurentii', upright dracaenas, especially those on a mini trunk, clivias and aglaonemas are among the plants that look good and won't get in the way of normal kitchen activities.

Practical pot plants

Many cooks like the idea of having culinary herbs on hand to pluck straight from pot to pot. Unfortunately, if you use herbs a great deal in your cooking, your herb plants will not remain attractive for long! So don't

expect your indoor herbs to keep the kitchen supplied, but they will create the right mood and aromas, and you can raid the plants for a leaf or two in an emergency. Nearly all herbs need good light, and the best place for them is by a bright window.

You can place individual pots on the windowsill, but it is more effective, and better for the plants, if you stand them all on a tray covering the length of the window and filled with gravel on which to stand the pots. Some, such as basil and pot marjoram, will need turning regularly to even up the growth, and regular pinching out of the growing tips is essential for many herbs. Unless you pinch out the growing tip, and later subsequent main shoots, basil will grow tall, flower and then deteriorate before you can harvest much of a crop. Marjoram needs to be pinched back regularly to keep it compact: the flowers are pretty, but an untamed plant will be too big and bushy for a windowsill.

Young plants of shrubs such as sage (*Salvia officinalis*) and rosemary (*Rosmarinus officinalis*) are inexpensive to buy and are worth growing as young pot plants. They will deteriorate indoors long before they become the large shrubs that you see in gardens, but they will enhance the kitchen for a season. If they are still alive and healthy the following spring, plant them in the garden, and buy another small plant for indoors.

Planting a herb windowbox

1. For an inexpensive improvised windowbox, use a polystyrene (styrofoam) trough. You can paint it to suit the decor.

2. Always insert a layer of drainage material, such as gravel and charcoal or expanded clay granules, before filling with potting compost (medium).

3. Choose small, bushy plants wherever possible. Some will eventually grow too tall, but you can usually restrict the height by repeatedly pinching out the growing tips.

OPPOSITE ABOVE: *Windowsill space is often limited, but kitchen shelves provide scope for many more plants, and a white-painted wall will reflect the available light and encourage growth.*

OPPOSITE BELOW: *Use trailers like this* **Philodendron scandens** *where its cascading stems won't get in the way. Near working surfaces, choose compact plants like this variegated* Tolmiea menziesii.

CENTRE RIGHT: *An indoor or outdoor windowbox full of herbs will not keep you supplied with all you need for culinary use, but it's a fun feature and may extend the season of fresh herbs when those outdoors are no longer available. This windowbox contains (from left to right) basil, thyme, parsley, rosemary and variegated apple mint.*

BELOW RIGHT: *The vacant space on top of cupboards can be used for low-growing or trailing plants, but bear in mind that light levels are often low, trailers may interfere with opening doors and watering can be difficult.*

BELOW FAR RIGHT: *Codiaeums usually do well in a kitchen provided you avoid a position exposed to cold draughts.*

Bedrooms

IF YOUR ENTHUSIASM FOR PLANTS OUTGROWS THE SPACE AVAILABLE IN

TRADITIONAL DISPLAY AREAS SUCH AS THE LIVING-ROOM AND KITCHEN,

OVERCOME PREJUDICE AND MAKE YOUR BEDROOM MORE BEAUTIFUL, TOO.

Many people are deterred from placing plants in their bedroom on the grounds that they are 'unhealthy'. However, plants will not deprive you of oxygen, and the reluctance to use them in the bedroom is no more than prejudice. You will probably find it a more restful place with the added greenery of a few plants, and you can even wake up to the perfume of stephanotis or hyacinths.

Bedrooms are often kept cooler than living-rooms, and this is an advantage for many plants. Winter-flowering plants, in particular, often last much longer in a cool atmosphere.

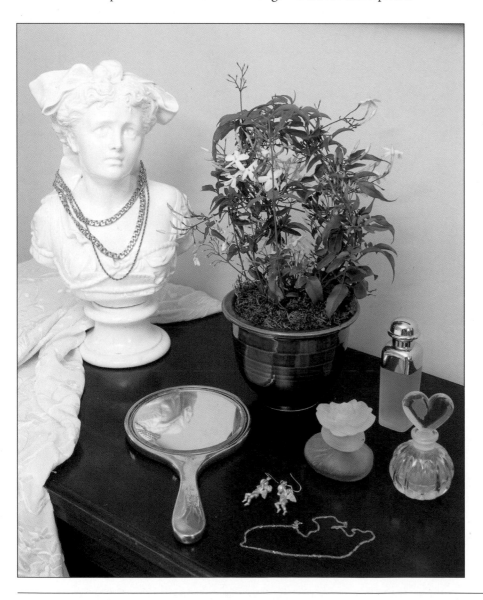

Suitable plants

Plants in bedrooms are probably viewed less than those in other parts of the house. Although we spend many hours there, most of them will be spent asleep, which means the plants are sometimes neglected.

Bedrooms are an excellent place for a collection of cacti and succulents, and for large individual specimens of tolerant foliage plants such as aspidistras and scindapsus (epipremnums), which are unlikely to become stressed if forgotten for a day or two.

If you can discipline yourself to water and mist them regularly, however, even delicate ferns will often do well because the air is usually more humid than in a hot living-room.

Fragrant plants can be especially pleasing, and the strongest scents will be appreciated beyond the bedroom itself if you leave the door open.

Bedside tables and dressing tables

Plants can add the finishing touch to a dressing table or a bedside table, but these are usually areas where natural light levels are low. Table lamps can display the plant to advantage after dark, but these do little for plant growth (and if too near, may scorch the plant). Be prepared to move your plants around, giving them a week or two at most in these positions, then rotate them with other plants that have had a spell in better light.

A place for plants to rest

Although you will want your bedroom to look well-designed and furnished with pretty or attractive plants, you may want to use a spare bedroom as a resting place for all those plants that are so perfect for a short time but border on the unattractive for the rest of the year. 'Resting' orchids and ephiphyllums, and tender primulas that have finished flowering, for example, are among the candidates for a light position in a bedroom. You can move them into a prominent position when they come into bloom again.

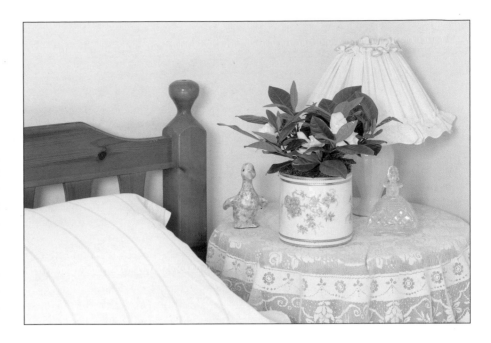

OPPOSITE ABOVE: *Instead of using air fresheners, wake up to the fragrance of real flowers, provided by plants such as this* Stephanotis floribunda.

OPPOSITE BELOW: *Enjoy the delicate perfume of* Jasminum polyanthum *as you sit at your dressing table. Dressing-table plants should be used at their prime, then moved to a lighter and more appropriate position to recuperate.*

ABOVE RIGHT: *If you adore the heady scent of gardenias, try one on your bedside table. When flowering has finished, move it to a lighter position.*

RIGHT: *Many bromeliads bought in bloom are discarded after flowering, so they can be used on a table well away from the window. This one is* Vriesea splendens, *with a distinctive flower spike that can be 60cm (2ft) long. The yellow* Celosia plumosa *is an inexpensive annual which can be used as a short-term houseplant for a few weeks.*

Bathrooms

BATHROOMS ARE NOT THE PARADISE FOR PLANTS THAT SOME PEOPLE THINK.

ALTHOUGH THE HUMIDITY IS OFTEN HIGH, THERE ARE DRAWBACKS TOO, SO

CHOOSE YOUR PLANTS WITH CARE.

The average bathroom has conditions that prevail nowhere else in the home: short periods of high temperature and high humidity contrasting with much longer spells of quite cool conditions (especially if the central heating is not kept on permanently), and because the windows are often small, poor natural light. The plants may also have to contend with the use of aerosols and sprays containing a variety of chemicals for personal care, and often a liberal dusting of talcum powder too. These are not conditions in which the majority of houseplants will thrive.

Good positions

Try to keep foliage out of reach of splashes from the bath and washbasin. Pots perched on the edge or back of the bath are in a precarious position, and the chances are that the light will also be poor.

Make the most of the windowsill, especially for flowering plants. Further into the room, use tough foliage plants such as aspidistras and asparagus ferns, perhaps in front of a mirror, where they will receive reflected light and the mirror will make the plants look larger.

Tolerant trailers such as ivies and *Philodendron scandens* look good hanging from a high shelf, perhaps framing a mirror.

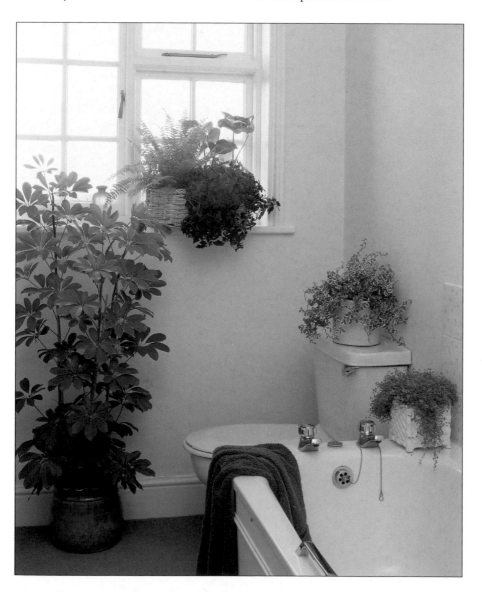

LEFT: *Plants may have to be concentrated near the window as bathrooms are not usually well illuminated with natural light, but by using plenty of plants on all available surfaces, the effect can be particularly pleasing.*

CARING FOR YOUR PLANTS

Bathroom plants need more regular grooming than those growing elsewhere. Leaf cleaning in particular should be done at least once a week. It is difficult to remove powder from plants with hairy leaves, so it is best to avoid these. If other plants become very coated with sprays or powder, try submerging the leaves briefly in water especially if there is so much foliage that it is tiring or impractical to wipe each leaf individually. If you splash soap, shampoo or toothpaste over a leaf, wipe it off immediately. If poor light is causing growth to arch towards the window, turn the plant regularly.

As soon as a plant appears to look unhappy, change it for another one. When the first one has recovered after a month or two in better conditions, rotate them again.

Use small flowering plants such as saintpaulias and kalanchoes on a make-up table or vanity unit, using attractive cache-pots that suit the setting. These will not make long-term bathroom plants, but they will look good for weeks before you have to move them on.

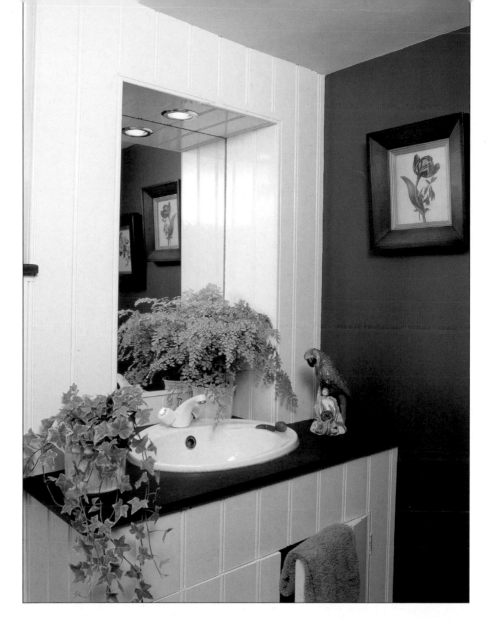

SUITABLE PLANTS

❧ The following plants generally do well:

❧ **Large plants**
Fatsia japonica, Monstera deliciosa and *Philodendron bipinnatifidum.*

❧ **Trailers**
Epipremnum aureum (syn. *Scindapsus aureus*)*, Philodendron scandens* and small-leaved ivies.

❧ **Bushy plants**
Aglaonema species and varieties, *Aspidistra elatior* and *Chamaedorea elegans* (syn. *Neanthe bella*).

❧ **Short-term flowering plants**
Chrysanthemum, cyclamen and *exacum.*

ABOVE RIGHT: *Plants as diverse as the hardy ivy and tricky* Asplenium capillus-veneris *can thrive in a bathroom. The ivy is good for low light levels, and the fern will appreciate the frequent spells of high humidity.*

RIGHT: **Philodendron scandens** *is a good choice for a trailer, while a spathiphyllum always looks elegant with its glossy green leaves and white sail-like flowers. Flowering plants, such as the cyclamen, can be brought in as short-term plants.*

FAR RIGHT: *Use trailers with imagination. Bathrooms usually have small windows and tend to be relatively gloomy, but by rotating the plants between rooms periodically you can feature attractive plant displays in all areas of the home.*

TROUBLE-SHOOTING

No matter how circumspect you are in selecting new plants, how carefully you check them for signs of ill-health, or how well you care for them, pests and diseases arrive unannounced. However, they should never be allowed to spoil your enjoyment of houseplants and with a little vigilance most should be easily kept under control.

Eliminating pests

EVERYONE GETS PESTS ON THEIR HOUSEPLANTS: BEGINNERS, EXPERTS AND

EVEN PROFESSIONALS. SOME, LIKE APHIDS, READILY ATTACK A WHOLE RANGE

OF PLANTS, OTHERS ARE MORE SELECTIVE AND TEND TO BE A PROBLEM ONLY

ON CERTAIN TYPES OF PLANT, OR IN PARTICULAR CONDITIONS. ALL NEED TO

BE DEALT WITH QUICKLY AND EFFECTIVELY.

Red spider mites
Red spider mites are so small that you can
hardly see them without a magnifying glass,
but, as this sick *Fatsia japonica* shows, an
infestation can be serious.

Aphids
Aphids are perhaps the most common and
troublesome pest, but are relatively easy to
control provided you act as soon as they
are detected.

Whitefly
Whitefly look like tiny white moths that often
rise up like a cloud when the plant is moved.
Although tiny, they gradually weaken the
plant, as this radermachera shows.

Mealy bugs
Mealy bugs are slow-moving and multiply less
rapidly than aphids, but they still weaken the
plant and can spread diseases.

Most pests fall into one of the three categories given below, so even if you do encounter a pest that you don't immediately recognize, you should be able to decide from this information which group it falls into, and choose an appropriate control.

Sap-suckers

The ubiquitous aphids are the biggest problem, and even if you win the first battle when you realize that an attack is under way, never let your guard down because there will always be new armies of aphids to take their place.

Aphids, and all sap-sucking insects, are important not only for the immediate damage they do, but also because of the long-term health risk to your plants. When aphids cluster on buds or the tips of shoots, leaves and flowers will often be distorted when they open, and because they tap into

the veins and 'blood' supply of the plant, they can easily transmit virus diseases from one plant to another. Always take aphids seriously, and take action before the population rapidly increases, as they can reproduce at a phenomenal rate.

Whitefly look like tiny moths and rise up in a cloud when disturbed. The nymphs (immature insects) are green to white and scale-like, turning yellow before emerging as an adult fly.

Red spider mites are tiny and the actual insects are easily missed, but you will notice their fine webs and yellowing, mottled leaves.

Control: almost all houseplant insecticides will control aphids, so choose one that is convenient to use, and has the right persistence taking into account your personal views on garden chemicals. You can buy some insecti-

cides that kill only aphids and leave beneficial insects unharmed, but in the home this is of marginal benefit. You don't have to worry about pollinating insects or natural predators as you might outdoors. Many strong insecticides are not suitable for use indoors, but you can take your plant outside to spray it. Alternatively, use one of the milder and less persistent ones – often based on natural substances like pyrethrum – more often.

Systemic insecticides that you water into the soil, or that are contained in impregnated sticks pushed into the compost, are easy to use indoors and protect the plant for weeks.

Pests like whitefly need repeated spraying with ordinary contact insecticides, so don't give up too soon.

Red spider mites dislike a humid atmosphere Once you've used the chemical control, regular misting to

Caterpillar damage
Caterpillars can be a problem on indoor plants as well as in the garden. Here one has attacked a pereskia.

Biological controls
A predatory mite – *Phytoseiulus persimilis* – can be used for red spider mite as a biological control. Here a leaf containing the parasite is being placed on a houseplant.

Nematode weevil control
There is now a natural control for vine weevil grubs – a microscopic parasitic nematode. Mix the culture with water and apply to the plants. Here a cyclamen is being dosed.

Vine weevil grubs
Vine weevil grubs are particularly troublesome because they eat the roots and the first you may know of the problem is when the plant collapses.

Using systemic insecticides
These special 'pins' release a systemic insecticide that is absorbed by the plant's roots, making the plant toxic to sap-sucking insects for weeks.

Controlling aphids
You may be able to reduce the population of insects such as aphids simply by swishing the plant in water.

create a humid atmosphere will please the plants and deter the mites.

Mealy bugs and other relatively stationary sap-sucking insects can be treated by dabbing them with a cotton swab dipped in alcohol. This will penetrate the waxy coat that protects them from most contact insectides. Otherwise try using a systemic insectide that will be carried in the sap.

Leaf eaters
Leaf eaters give themselves away soon after arrival, by the tell-tale chunks missing from leaves. Fortunately, most of the these pests are large and easily seen, and on the whole control is relatively simple.

Control: large pests that remain on the plant, such as caterpillars, slugs and snails, can usually be picked off by hand (remove the whole leaf if in-fested). Chemical control is hardly ever necessary indoors, but in a conservatory you may want to use slug bait (protect it under pieces of broken pot if you have pets).

Those insects that feed at night and hide during the day, such as earwigs, present a bigger problem. Most household crawling insect powders and sprays will control these if you use them around the area where the plants are. If you don't want to use an insecticide, leave small traps made from matchboxes, left slightly open and filled with litter such as chopped straw. Check these each morning and destroy any pests that you find.

Root chewers
The problem with root pests is that you are unlikely to know of their existence until the plant collapses, by which time it's often too late.

A number of pests affect the roots, from some types of aphids to the grubs of insects such as weevils. If a plant looks sick, fails to grow properly, or starts to collapse, and there is no obvious cause such as overwatering or underwatering, remove the plant from its pot and shake off the compost (potting soil). Examine the roots: if there are grubs or other pests, that's the likely cause; if you find none but the roots are sparse or rotting, a fungus disease is the more likely cause.

Control: if you have taken the plant out of its pot for examination, shake the compost off the roots and dip them into an insecticidal solution before repotting in fresh compost. Your plant may then recover. Drench the compost in nearby pots with an insecticidal solution as a further precaution, though results may be variable.

Dealing with diseases

PLANT DISEASES CAN BE DISFIGURING AND EVEN FATAL, SO ALWAYS TAKE
THEM SERIOUSLY. IF YOU CAN'T CONTROL THEM BY PICKING OFF THE
AFFECTED LEAVES, RAPID RESORT TO A FUNGICIDE MAY BE THE BEST SOLU-
TION. IF A VIRUS STRIKES, IT MAY BE BETTER TO SACRIFICE THE PLANT TO
THE BIN RATHER THAN RISK THE INFECTION SPREADING TO OTHER PLANTS.

Leaf spot
Leaf spots are quite common, and are
caused by various fungi. If just a few leaves
are affected, pick them off then spray the
rest of the plant as a precaution.

Fungus diseases are often difficult
to identify accurately and many
different species of fungi can cause
similar symptoms. Fortunately, a scientific identification of the exact fungus is not necessary in order to go
about controlling it. The chemicals
used to control each main group of
diseases are largely effective against all
the organisms likely to be responsible
– but don't assume that all fungicides
are equally effective against all fungus
diseases. Always read the label to
check what disease a particular chemical is most effective against.

Leaf spots

Various fungi and bacteria cause leaf
spots. If tiny black specks can be seen
on the affected surface, they are likely
to be the spore-bearing bodies of a
fungus, so a fungicide is likely to be
effective. If no specks can be detected
it might be a bacterial problem,
though a fungicide might still be of
some help.

Control: prune off and destroy the
affected leaves. Water with a systemic
fungicide, and avoid misting too frequently. Increase ventilation if the
weather permits.

Root rots

The first sign of a root rot is usually
the sudden collapse of a seemingly
healthy plant. The leaves turn brown
or black, and curl up. The entire plant
may wilt. This is almost always the
result of overwatering.

Control: if the plant has not already
deteriorated too far, try drying it out.
However, there is usually little that
can be done at this stage.

Sooty mould

The fungus covers the leaves, often the
back but sometimes the front, with a
black growth that looks like soot. It
does not directly harm the plants but
looks unsightly.

Fungal diseases
The protective sleeve of this newly
purchased saintpaulia disguised the fact
that it is infected with *Botrytis cinerea*.

This grey-brown mould develops on dead or
damaged plants, and can be caused by lack
of ventilation.

Sooty mould
Sooty mould is a fungus that grows on the sugary substance excreted by aphids and other sap-suckers. If you control the pests you will eliminate the disease, which is unsightly but not particularly harmful.

Mildew
Various kinds of mildew affect houseplants, and begonias are particularly prone to them. Control is difficult once the disease is well established, but various fungicides are useful for early and preventative treatment.

Control: sooty mould is a fungus that lives on the 'honeydew' (excrement) left by aphids and whitefly. When this food disappears so will the sooty mould, so eliminate the insects that are the prime cause.

Mildews
There are various kinds of mildew, the powdery types being the most common. Evidence of the disease is seen as a white, powdery deposit, almost as if the leaf has been sprinkled with flour. The problem starts in one or two areas but quickly radiates out and can soon engulf the whole leaf. Some plants, such as begonias, are more prone to mildew than others.

Control: pick off the affected leaves at an early stage, then use a fungicide to limit its spread. Increase ventilation, and reduce the humidity around the plant – at least until the disease is under control.

Using fungicides
If you need to use a fungicide, you can use those developed for outdoor plants by mixing a small amount and using it in a hand-pumped mister.

Viruses
The main symptoms of virus diseases are stunted or distorted growth, irregular yellow blotches on foliage and streaked petals on flowering plants. They are easily transmitted by sap-sucking insects such as aphids, and can even be carried on the knives used to take cuttings.

There is no effective control and, apart from the rare cases where the plants are cultivated for the variegation caused by the virus, the plants are best destroyed.

Disorders and deficiencies

NOT ALL TROUBLES ARE CAUSED BY PESTS AND DISEASES. SOMETIMES PHY-

SIOLOGICAL PROBLEMS SUCH AS CHILLS AND COLD DRAUGHTS, OR NUTRI-

TIONAL DEFICIENCIES, CAN BE THE CAUSE.

Tracking down a physiological problem calls for a bit of detective work. The descriptions of some common problems described here will help to pinpoint some potential causes, but be prepared to look for anything that has disturbed the usual routine – has the plant been moved, watered more or less heavily, has the weather become much colder, have you turned the central heating on but not increased humidity or ventilation? By piecing together the various clues you can often deduce probable causes, and thereby work out what you can do to avoid a repetition.

Temperature

Most houseplants will tolerate cool but frost-free temperatures if they have to. It is sudden changes of temperature or icy draughts in a warm room that cause most problems.

If leaves drop it may be due to low temperature. This often happens with newly bought plants that have been on display outdoors or chilled on the way home. Leaves that look shrivelled and slightly translucent may have been touched by frost.

Hardy plants like *Euonymus japonicus* may drop their leaves if kept too warm in winter. Berries are also likely to fall prematurely if the temperature is kept too high.

Light and sun

Plants that need a high light intensity will become elongated and drawn if the illumination is poor, and leaves and flower stalks will be drawn towards the window. Lop-sided growth is another indication of inadequate

Neglect
This plant is clearly showing signs of stress and lack of nutrients. It may be best to discard a plant in this state.

Sun scorch
Plants that are not adapted to grow in very strong light are easily scorched by strong sunlight intensified by a glass window. This dieffenbachia is suffering from scorch.

light. If you can't move the plant into a lighter position, try turning the pot round by 45 degrees each day (put a tiny mark on the pot as a reminder of whether you've turned it).

Light is usually a good thing, but direct sunlight, intensified through glass, will often scorch leaves – the effect will be brown, papery areas on the leaf. Patterned glass is a particular problem as it can act like a magnifying glass, causing dry brown patches where the rays have been concentrated.

Humidity
Dry air can cause leaf tips to go brown and papery on vulnerable plants.

Watering
Too little water is the most likely cause of wilting and collapse, if the compost (potting soil) feels very dry to the touch. If the plant collapses and the compost feels very wet, or water is standing in the saucer or cache-pot, suspect overwatering.

Feeding
Pale leaves and short, stunted growth may be due to lack of fertilizer in the

Effects of overwatering
Yellowing lower leaves are often a sign of overwatering, but may also be due to a chill if it happens in winter. This is a *Fatshedera lizei* beginning to show signs of overwatering.

Aerosol scorch

A plant can also be damaged by aerosol sprays (even one containing an insecticide intended for houseplants). This dieffenbachia has dropped many of its leaves, and others are scorched, because an insecticidal aerosol was used too close to the plant.

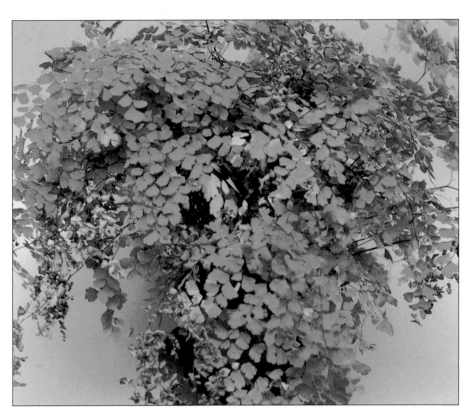

Effects of dry air

Dry air is a particular problem for most ferns. This adiantum is showing the signs of low humidity.

compost (potting soil). Try liquid feeding for a quick boost. Specific plants, such as citrus fruits and rhododendrons, may show signs of iron deficiency (yellowing leaves) if grown in an alkaline compost. Feed with a chelated (sequestered) iron and next time you repot use an ericaceous compost (specially developed for lime-hating plants).

Bud drop

Bud drop is often caused by dry compost (potting soil) or dry air, but sometimes it is due to the plant being moved to a different position or turned once the buds have formed. (Zygocactus is an example of a plant that resents having to re-orientate its buds to light from a different direction.)

Dehydration

This thunbergia shows the classic symptoms of a dehydrated plant. The very dry compost (potting soil) is confirmation of the cause. The best treatment is to stand the pot in a bowl of water for several hours, until the compost is thoroughly wet. Peat (peat moss) composts are particularly difficult to rewet once they have dried out completely, but a few drops of mild household detergent added to the water will help to rewet it.

Bud drop

Bud drop is often caused by dry root, overwatering, or by moving a plant once the flower buds have formed.

Wilting and worse

WHEN A PLANT WILTS OR APPEARS TO COLLAPSE, IT'S TIME TO TAKE DRASTIC

ACTION. THE FIRST PRIORITY IS TO DECIDE WHAT'S WRONG, THEN, IF

POSSIBLE, TO APPLY FIRST AID MEASURES WITHOUT DELAY TO BRING THE

PLANT BACK TO HEALTH.

First aid for a dry plant

1. If the leaves of a plant have started to wilt like this, the compost (potting soil) is probably too dry. Feel it first – overwatering also causes wilting.

2. Stand the pot in a bowl or bucket of water and leave it until the air bubbles have ceased to rise.

3. It will take some hours for the water to revive the plant. In the meantime, help the plant further by misting the leaves with water from time to time.

4. Once the plant has revived, remove it from the bowl and stand it in a cool place out of direct sunlight for at least a day.

Wilting and collapse are a signal that something is drastically wrong. If you ignore this warning, you may lose the plant. Plants usually wilt for one of three reasons:

- Too much water.
- Too little water.
- Insects or a disease affecting the roots.

The first two will usually be obvious: if the compost (potting soil) is hard and dry, underwatering is the likely cause: if there is water standing in the cache-pot or saucer, or if the compost oozes water, overwatering is almost certainly the cause.

If the compost seems neither over-watered nor underwatered, check the base of the plant just above compost level. If the stem looks black or rotten, a fungus disease is the likely cause and the plant is best discarded.

If none of the above symptoms are present, remove the plant from its pot and shake off some of the soil. If many of the roots are soft or black and decaying, a root disease is the likely cause. Look also for grubs or other insects around the roots. The larvae of beetles such as weevils can sometimes cause a plant to collapse.

First aid for root pests or diseases
It will be very difficult to revive a plant with a severe root rot, but you can try drenching the compost with a fungicide, then after a couple of hours letting it dry out on absorbent paper. If the root system is badly damaged it may be worth repotting it in sterilized compost first, after removing as much of the old soil as possible.

Some soil pests, such as root aphids, can be controlled if drenched with an insecticide. Wine weevil grubs and other serious soil pests are not so easy to control. Try shaking the old soil off the roots, dusting them with an insecticidal powder, then repotting in fresh, sterilized compost. If the damage is not too extensive the plant may survive once it has had time to make new growth.

First aid for a wet plant

1. Knock the plant out of its pot. If it does not come out easily, invert the plant while holding the compost (potting soil) in with one hand, and knock the rim of the pot on a hard surface.

2. Wrap the root-ball in several layers of absorbent paper.

3. Stand the plant in a warm place, out of direct sunlight, with more absorbent paper wrapped around the root-ball. Change the paper periodically if it is still drawing moisture from the compost.

OTHER POSSIBLE CAUSES OF COLLAPSE

🌂 Plants may collapse for physiological reasons:

🌂 Cold air at night, especially in winter, may cause some plants to collapse, especially if they have been kept warm during the day.

🌂 Strong, hot sunshine through glass will make many plants wilt. Usually they recover when given cooler, shadier conditions.

🌂 Hot, dry air will have a similar effect on some plants, such as the more delicate ferns.

🌂 Poor light will eventually cause a plant to exhaust itself. But this is likely to be a gradual process, much less rapid than collapse caused by watering problems or pests.

4. Continue until the compost has dried out, but do not let it become completely dry. Repot and water only very cautiously for the next week.

Glossary

Aerial root A root that grows from the stem above ground level. Plants such as philodendrons use them to assist climbing, as well as to absorb moisture and nutrients.

Alkaline compost A growing medium containing lime, and having a high pH level.

Annual A plant that lives for only one year.

Bract A modified leaf, often brightly coloured and serving to attract pollinating insects to insignificant flowers that lack bright petals.

Bromeliad A member of the *Bromeliaceae* family. Most are ephiphytic, and the leaves usually form a rosette.

Bulb Although the term is often used to include corms and tubers, a bulb is a structure consisting of modified leaves that protects the next season's embryo shoots and flowers.

Bulbil A small bulb that forms above ground on a few plants. Bulbils can be removed and potted up to grow into normal bulbs.

Callus A growth of corky tissue that forms over a wound, sealing and healing it.

Capillary mat An absorbent mat that holds a lot of water. Plants placed on it can draw up moisture by capillary action.

Chlorophyll The green colouring pigment in plants which enables them to manufacture food from sunlight (photosynthesize).

Chlorosis An unhealthy yellowing of the foliage, usually caused by a deficiency of iron or other trace elements.

Often appears in lime-hating plants which have been grown in an alkaline medium.

Compost (potting soil) The medium in which pot plants are grown.

Corm A swollen stem base that usually remains underground and stores food during the dormant season. If cut across, no distinct layers of leaves can be seen, unlike a bulb.

Crocks Pieces of broken clay pot (also known as shards), placed over the drainage hole of a clay pot to prevent the compost (potting soil) from being washed through the hole.

Crown The point at which stem and roots meet.

Dormant period The time when growth slows down and the plant needs less warmth and water. Some plants have no discernible dormant period, but with others – such as cyclamen – it is pronounced.

Epiphyte A plant that grows above ground level, usually in trees. Epiphytes are not parasites and only use their host for physical support.

Foliar feed A quick-acting liquid fertilizer that can be absorbed through the leaves as well as the roots.

Genus A group of species with enough common characteristics to group them together like a 'family'.

Hardy Frost-tolerant.

Hormone, rooting hormone An organic compound that stimulates a cutting into forming roots.

Humidifier A device for raising the humidity in a room. Sometimes a tray of evaporating water is used, but more sophisticated humidifiers are electrically powered.

Hydroponics A method of growing plants in nutrient solutions, without compost (potting soil).

Loam-based compost (potting soil) A soil mix in which the main ingredient is sterilized loam, to which peat (peat moss), sand and fertilizer are added.

Lux The scientific unit by which light levels are measured.

Offset A small plant that is produced alongside its parent.

Peat-based compost (peat-moss-based potting soil) A soil mix in which peat is the main ingredient. Sometimes sand and other substances are added, and the mixture always includes fertilizers and something to neutralize the acidity of the peat. Peat substitutes, such as coir, are increasingly used to avoid depletion of natural peat reserves.

Perennial A plant that lives for more than two years.

Perlite An inert growing medium, sometimes used as a compost (potting soil) additive or for rooting cuttings.

Petiole A leaf stalk.

pH A scale expressing the degree of acidity or alkalinity of a substance. It runs from 0 to 14, 7 being technically neutral, though most plants prefer a pH of about 6.5. Above 7 is alkaline, below 7 is acid.

Photosynthesis The mechanism by which plants convert sunlight into energy.

Pot-bound A term used to describe a plant whose growth is being inhibited by roots that have filled the pot.

Relative humidity The amount of water contained in the air at a particular temperature. It is calculated against the maximum amount of water that could be held in the air at that temperature.

Resting period *see* **Dormant period**

Rhizome A horizontal stem, on the surface or just below, and a form of storage organ.

Root-ball A mass of roots and compost (potting soil) together.

Sphagnum moss A moss belonging to the genus *Sphagnum,* found in boggy places and capable of holding a large amount of water.

Tuber A swollen underground stem or root used by plants to store food during the dormant period.

Vermiculite An inert growing medium, sometimes used as a compost (potting soil) additive or for rooting cuttings.

Index of common plant names

Index